ARCHITECTURE EXAM REVIEW

Site Planning and Building Design
Graphic Divisions

Third Edition

David Kent Ballast, AIA

Professional Publications, Inc
Belmont, CA

Managing Editor: Jessica R. Whitney-Holden
Copy Editor: Lisa Rominger
Book Designer: Charles P. Oey
Typesetter: Cathy Schrott
Proofreader: Jessica R. Whitney-Holden
Cover Designer: Chuck Oey and Yvonne Sartain

Architecture Exam Review: Site Planning and Building Design Graphic Divisions
Third Edition

Printed in the United States of America

ISBN: 1-888577-42-8

Professional Publications, Inc.
1250 Fifth Avenue, Belmont, CA 94002
(650) 593-9119
www.ppi2pass.com

Current printing of this edition: 1

Library of Congress Cataloging-in-Publication Data
Ballast, David Kent
    Architecture exam review: site planning and building design
    graphic divisions / David Kent Ballast. -- 3rd ed.
        p.   cm.
    ISBN 1-888577-42-8 (pbk.)
    1. Architecture--United States--Examinations--Study guides.
    I. Title.
    NA123.B36   1999
    720'.76--dc21
                                                                99-24759
                                                                CIP

Contents

Introduction

This guide has been written to help you review for the graphic divisions of the Architect Registration Examination (A.R.E.). The companion volumes on structural and nonstructural topics are aimed at helping you review for the multiple-choice divisions and also provide additional help with the graphic divisions. In this guide, the format of each vignette in the graphic divisions is described along with some of the general grading criteria. A sample paper-and-pencil version of each vignette is given so you can practice your skills with constraints similar to those you will encounter on the actual examination. Example solutions are also included to help you see what is considered a good and a poor solution. Even though the exam is completely computer based, the samples in this guide will prepare you for what to expect and how to approach each vignette.

THE ARCHITECT REGISTRATION EXAMINATION

The Architect Registration Examination is a uniform test administered to candidates who wish to become licensed architects after they have served their required internships. It is given in all fifty states, nine Canadian provinces, and five other jurisdictions.

The A.R.E. has been developed to protect the health, safety, and welfare of the public by testing a candidate's entry-level competence to practice architecture. Its content relates as closely as possible to situations encountered in practice. It tests for the kinds of knowledge, skills, and abilities required of an architect, with particular emphasis on those services that affect public health, safety, and welfare. In order to accomplish these objectives, the exam tests for (1) knowledge in specific subject areas, (2) the ability to make decisions, (3) the ability to consolidate and use information to solve a problem, and (4) the ability to coordinate the activities of others on the building team. It also includes some project management questions.

The A.R.E. is developed jointly by the National Council of Architectural Registration Boards (NCARB) and the Committee of Canadian Architectural Councils (CCAC) with the assistance of the Educational Testing Service (ETS). The ETS helps with production, distribution, and scoring; it also serves as a consultant for testing format and writing of questions.

The examination is now a totally computer-administered and -graded test. The NCARB offers the examination six days a week at a network of test centers across North America. Candidates can take the exam in any order on any day and spread out the sessions to fit their schedules. The results are scored by computer and are available much more quickly than they were in the past. If the candidate fails a division, he or she must wait six months to retake that division.

For the multiple-choice portions of the examination, the computer administers an initial set of questions. Based on the candidate's responses, the computer decides if the candidate has a mastery of the material or not. If the responses indicate a borderline candidate, the computer will administer an additional set of questions to verify competency. This process continues until the maximum length of the test has been reached, at which time the candidate is graded either "pass" or "fail."

For the graphic portions of the exam, the computer uses a complex method of grading based on categories of acceptable, unacceptable, and indeterminate responses. Along with point values for design criteria, the computer uses the responses and grading categories to score the solution.

Even though the A.R.E. is now computer administered, the knowledge and skills it tests for are the same as they have always been. Therefore, you will find that this guide and the related structural and nonstructural volumes are still valuable parts of your exam preparation. Although there is no substitute for a good formal education and broad-based experience provided by your internship with a practicing architect, this review guide will help direct your study efforts to increase your chances of passing the A.R.E.

To apply for registration you should obtain the requirements for registration from the board in the state, province, or territory where you want to be registered initially. The exact requirements vary from one jurisdiction to another, so you need to contact your local board.

The National Council of Architectural Registration Boards has established a World Wide Web site that provides current information about the exam, education requirements, training, examination procedures, and NCARB reciprocity services. Included are sample scenarios of the computer-based examination process and examples of costs associated with taking the new computer-based exam. The website address is www.ncarb.org. Additional information is also available from this publisher at www.ppi2pass.com.

EXAMINATION FORMAT

The A.R.E. is designed to protect the health, safety, and welfare of the public by regulating the practice of architecture. It does this by testing to see if a qualified candidate has the knowledge, skills, and abilities to perform the services required of an entry-level architect. To this end, the examination is divided into several divisions, which test various areas of architectural knowledge and problem-solving ability.

The examination is administered throughout the year at test sites across the country and currently consists of nine divisions. The divisions are as follows.

- Pre-Design
- Site Planning
- Building Planning
- Building Technology
- General Structures

- Lateral Forces
- Mechanical and Electrical
- Materials and Methods
- Construction Documents and Services

Unlike with the previous exam, you may now schedule any division of the A.R.E. at any time you choose and in any order. You can take one division at a time to allow for adequate preparation and spread out exam costs, or you can group divisions together. If you fail a division, you may repeat that division six months after your unsuccessful attempt.

The time allotted for each section varies, but most candidates do not need the entire time to complete the multiple-choice divisions. The graphic divisions are scheduled for a fixed length of time and include breaks.

For the graphic portions of the exam that this guide covers, there are a total of fifteen vignettes, six for Site Planning and nine for Building Design. The Building Design division is broken into two parts: Building Planning and Building Technology.

SITE PLANNING

The Site Planning portion of the exam consists of six short vignettes that require you to analyze program requirements and existing conditions and design a workable solution for each one. These vignettes are site design, site zoning, site parking, site analysis, site section, and grading. The first vignette gives you a program and requires that you lay out two buildings and other site components into a coherent concept. The other five vignettes test specific areas of knowledge. The first vignette is designed to be completed in about an hour, whereas the other vignettes are designed to be completed in about one half hour each.

The problems test your ability to perform common site design tasks such as manipulating contours, laying out parking, understanding zoning restrictions, arranging building and natural elements on a site, and working with various kinds of site restrictions. The site design vignettes are laid out on the computer screen using the built-in CAD program.

Vignette Descriptions

Vignette 1, Site Design. This vignette requires that you prepare a schematic site plan that is responsive to various programmatic, functional, orientation, and setback requirements provided in the program. You are given a program, a site plan, a conceptual building footprint for two buildings, and other site factors. You must understand how to accommodate pedestrian and vehicular circulation, land utilization, views, and other design considerations.

Vignette 2, Site Zoning. This vignette requires that you understand the cross-sectional building area limitations imposed by zoning and other setback restrictions. You must draw a profile line on a cross-sectional grid that includes the existing site grade and the maximum buildable envelope above grade.

Vignette 3, Parking. This vignette requires that you lay out parking spaces and access drives to satisfy given program requirements. You are given a site plan with existing surface features and any buildings that need to be served as well as a program of requirements. You must demonstrate your understanding of site-related requirements and limitations that influence the design and layout of vehicular parking spaces and the areas required for circulation and maneuvering.

Vignette 4, Site Analysis. This vignette tests your understanding of site-related requirements and limitations that influence the subdivision of land and the delineation of areas suitable for building construction and other surface improvements. Given a site plan and program, you are required to divide an existing lot into two lots and to indicate areas suitable for building construction and other surface improvements.

Vignette 5, Site Section. This vignette requires that you understand how site sections or profiles are affected by site design requirements. You are given a program and an existing site profile and must manipulate the profile and place two structures and one other site element to achieve the objectives stated in the program.

Vignette 6, Grading. This vignette tests your ability to manipulate site topography to achieve stated objectives. You are given an existing site plan with contours and a program and must "regrade" the site to satisfy the requirements of the problem.

The sample vignettes in this book and basic site planning information in the companion book, *Architecture Exam Review, Volume II: Nonstructural Topics*, should give you a feel for the type of problems you will have to solve.

Examination Grading

For each vignette, a set of grading criteria is established that relates specifically to that vignette. The computer uses a complex method of grading that employs a system of three ordered categories for each element that the test writers consider important. These categories include clearly acceptable, clearly unacceptable, and indeterminate. For example, if the computer detects that you have located a setback line the correct distance from the property line, that portion of the vignette receives an acceptable score. Groups of elements are weighted and combined in a complex scoring method to arrive at an overall score for the vignette. This scoring method applies objective criteria to the grading while allowing for the relative importance of certain features and tolerances for some aspects of the solution.

BUILDING DESIGN

The Building Design portion of the A.R.E. is divided into the Building Planning division and the Building Technology division, and it tests the candidate's ability to solve basic design problems such as space planning, mechanical and electrical system integration, structural planning, and accessibility layout.

Each of the nine vignettes is designed to test a particular area of knowledge and skill. The vignette format tests examinees' knowledge and skill levels by having each vignette focus on a particular task that practicing architects must know. This guide provides one sample for each of the vignettes along with a sample passing and failing solution. For more information on the Building Design division and another sample schematic design vignette, refer to the companion volume, *Architecture Exam Review, Volume II: Nonstructural Topics*.

Test Format

The Building Planning division consists of three vignettes: Block Diagram, Interior Layout, and Schematic Design. The Building Technology division consists of six vignettes: Building Section, Structural Layout, Accessibility—Ramp, Mechanical and Electrical, Stair Design, and Roof Plan. The Schematic Design vignette is the longest and requires you to design a small, two-story building based on a program and code requirements. All of the vignettes are completed on the computer using the proprietary CAD program developed by NCARB.

The recommended completion times for each vignette are as follows.

Block Diagram	1 hour
Interior Layout	3/4 hour
Schematic Design	4 hours
Building Section	1 hour
Structural Layout	3/4 hour
Accessibility—Ramp	3/4 hour
Mechanical and Electrical	1 hour
Stair Design	1 hour
Roof Plan	3/4 hour

Vignette Descriptions

Vignette 1, Block Diagram. This vignette provides you with a list of spaces for a given building, a bubble diagram, and some zoning and building code requirements. From that information you must develop a schematic block diagram on a given site, including basic site planning elements and required access connections.

Vignette 2, Interior Layout. This vignette tests your understanding of principles of design and accessibility that govern basic interior space planning. You are given a background floor plan, a program, and code requirements. You must plan the required spaces, including furniture, and show access to those spaces.

Vignette 3, Schematic Design. This vignette requires that you produce a two-story floor plan for a small building given a site plan, a program, and code requirements. You must satisfy the requirements of the program and code while addressing relevant features and limitations of the site.

Vignette 4, Building Section. This vignette requires that you develop a schematic section of a two-story building given the partial floor plans where the section is cut. Additional information includes building materials, structural systems, frost depth, mechanical system information, and heights and elevations of some building elements.

You must accurately draw the section that represents the given floor plans, while showing how you integrate structural elements, mechanical systems, and electrical systems. You must indicate appropriate footing and foundation depths and sizes, bearing walls as indicated on the plan, beams, and correct thicknesses for the given floor and roof assemblies. Roof slopes for drainage and parapets must be shown. Rated assemblies and fire dampers may also be part of the problem.

Vignette 5, Structural Layout. This vignette provides you with a floor plan of a small building and requires that you sketch a structural system using the graphic conventions given in order to meet the requirements of the problem. The structural system includes columns, bearing walls, and roof structure and may include simple foundation indications.

You must indicate an appropriate structural system with reasonable spacing of beams and joists given the spans and layout of the building. All the structural elements necessary for structural continuity must be shown so all loads are carried from the roof through all structural elements to the foundation.

Vignette 6, Accessibility—Ramp. This vignette tests your understanding of accessibility requirements as they relate to the design of ramp and stair systems. You are given a base plan, a program, and code requirements and must design a stair and ramp system connecting two floor elevations.

Vignette 7, Mechanical and Electrical. This vignette provides you with a background drawing, a program, code requirements, and a lighting diagram and requires that you complete a reflected ceiling plan by placing the ceiling grid and arranging the mechanical and electrical system components within it. The problem can include considerations for structural element sizes, duct sizes and types, footcandle levels, fire dampers, rated vertical shafts, placement of diffusers, and mechanical system requirements.

Vignette 8, Stair Design. This vignette tests your understanding of the three-dimensional nature of stair design and of the basic functional and code issues involved. You are given partial background floor plans of two levels, a building section, a program, and code requirements and must complete a floor plan with a stair system.

Vignette 9, Roof Plan. The roof plan vignette requires that you demonstrate your understanding of basic concepts related to roof design by completing the roof plan for a small building. You are given the outline of the roof, a background floor plan, and a program. You must complete the roof plan by indicating slopes, directions and elevations, and the locations of roof accessories and equipment.

Grading

As with the graphic site design vignettes, the building planning and technology vignettes are graded by the computer using a complex method of evaluation of individual responses to particular parts of each vignette. As with the old paper-and-pencil test, small errors will not cause a solution to fail if it is evident that the candidate has demonstrated an understanding of how to solve the major criteria of the problem.

TEST MATERIALS

You do not need and are not allowed to bring to the test site any reference materials, scratch paper, or calculators. Scratch paper is provided by the proctor and must be returned when leaving the exam room. A calculator function is provided on the computer terminal.

PRACTICE SOFTWARE

When you become eligible to take the graphic portions of the exam, you will have the opportunity to receive practice software from NCARB's test administration consultant at no additional charge. Although you are given time before each of the graphic divisions to practice with the software, you should get this practice software to become familiar with how the various tools for each vignette are used.

1

Site Planning

SITE DESIGN

A developer plans to build a video store, restaurant, deck, and parking area on the site shown on the following page. You must develop a schematic site plan based on the program that includes legal requirements and other site influences. You must place the buildings, deck, parking area, vehicular access and service drives, pedestrian walkways, and vegetation according to the following program.

1. Locate a one-story, 20 ft high restaurant close to the wetlands area.

2. Locate a one-story, 15 ft high video store close to the intersection of Stuart Street and 5th Avenue.

3. Draw a 1500 ft² outdoor dining deck for the restaurant.

4. The restaurant deck must have a view of the wetlands area.

5. The view of the service entrance of the restaurant shall be blocked from both streets and from the site to the south.

6. The entrance of the restaurant shall receive noonday summer sun.

7. The restaurant deck shall be blocked from the prevailing winds by trees or buildings as appropriate.

8. Draw a parking area to accommodate 20 cars.

- Provide an area to accommodate the required number of spaces and a 25 ft wide access aisle.
- Use 90°, 10 ft × 20 ft standard spaces and assume that the space provided allows for accessible parking spaces that will be used for *both* the video store and restaurant.

- Locate the parking area near the video store within the building limit lines. Parking for the restaurant is accommodated by an existing lot on the property immediately to the south.
- Delineation of individual parking spaces is not required.

9. Connect the parking area, video store, restaurant entrance, parking area south of the property, and 5th Avenue with a continuous pedestrian walkway. The restaurant deck may be considered part of the walkway system.

10. Draw vehicular circulation on the site to access the parking area and the service entrance to the restaurant. All drives shall be 20 ft wide.

- The service drive must not pass through the parking area.
- No turnaround for service vehicles is required.
- Only one curb cut on 5th Avenue is allowed, no closer than 140 ft from the south curb line of Stuart Street.

11. The following general conditions also apply:

- No built improvement can occur within the setbacks, except that driveways and sidewalks can cross setbacks to connect to public walks and streets.
- Provide a 30 ft setback from the property line adjacent to the wetlands area.
- Assume a 50 ft height for all trees.
- No more than five existing trees may be removed or disturbed.

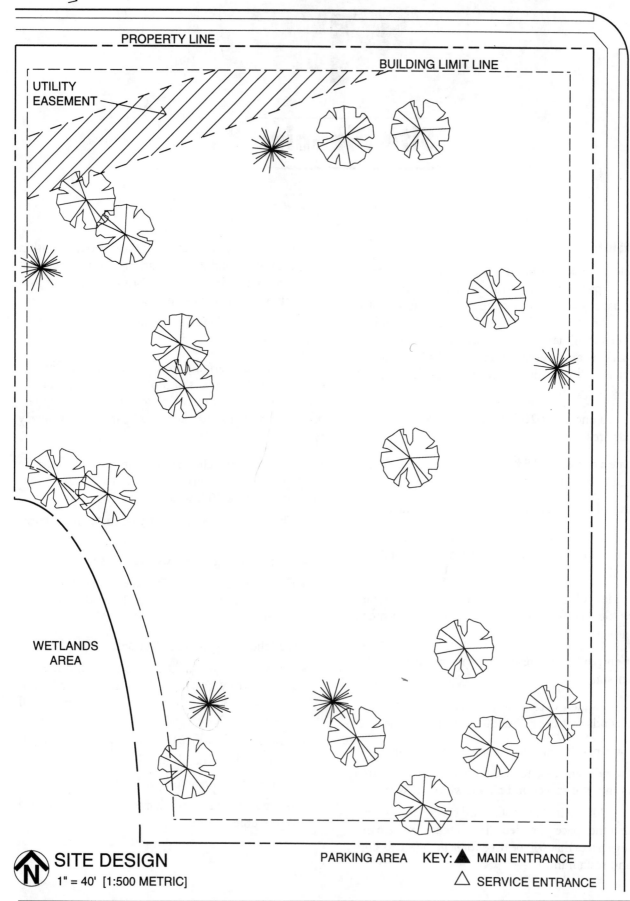

WINDS

STUART STREET

PROPERTY LINE

BUILDING LIMIT LINE

UTILITY
EASEMENT

5TH AVENUE

WETLANDS
AREA

SITE DESIGN
1" = 40' [1:500 METRIC]

PARKING AREA   KEY: ▲ MAIN ENTRANCE
△ SERVICE ENTRANCE

SITE ZONING

The drawing on the next page shows a site plan of two lots and a cross section grid. You must draw a cross section of the existing site grading at the section indicated and draw on the grid the maximum buildable envelope at the section according to the following requirements.

1. On the grid below the site plan, draw the profile of the existing site grade at section A–A.

2. On the grid at section A–A, draw the profile of the maximum buildable envelope allowed by the following restrictions:

- The side setback along the property line between Lot A and Lot B is 15 ft (4.6 m).
- The side setback along Side Street is 10 ft (3 m).

- The side setback along the south property line of Lot B is 20 ft (6.1 m).
- The maximum building height limit within 40 ft (12.2 m) of the Side Street property line is 30 ft (9.1 m) above the north building line.
- The maximum building height of any portion of a building on Lot A is 75 ft (22.9 m) above the average grade level at the building line.
- The maximum building height of structures on Lot B is 60 ft (18.3 m) above the bench mark elevation.
- The maximum building envelope for solar access is limited to an elevation defined by a 35° line rising from north to south beginning at a point 20 ft (6.1 m) above the building line at grade.

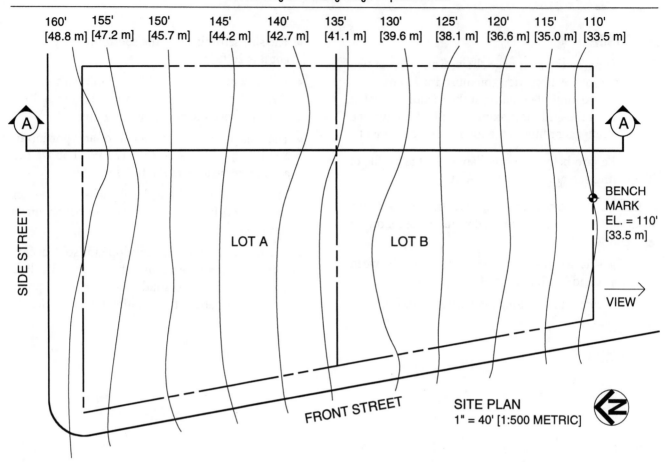

160'	155'	150'	145'	140'	135'	130'	125'	120'	115'	110'
[48.8 m]	[47.2 m]	[45.7 m]	[44.2 m]	[42.7 m]	[41.1 m]	[39.6 m]	[38.1 m]	[36.6 m]	[35.0 m]	[33.5 m]

SIDE STREET

LOT A   LOT B

BENCH
MARK
EL. = 110'
[33.5 m]

VIEW

FRONT STREET

SITE PLAN
1" = 40' [1:500 METRIC]

N

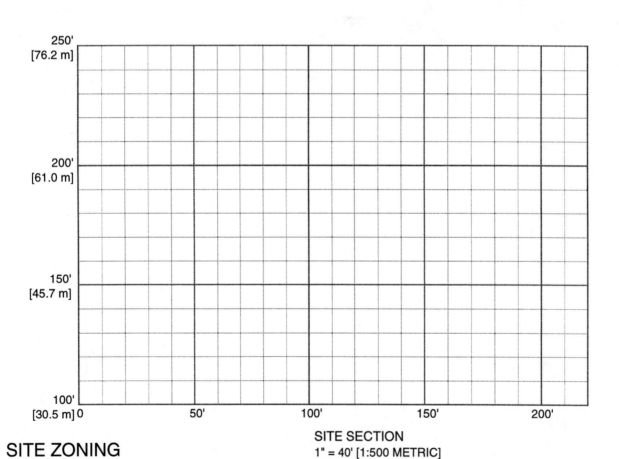

250'
[76.2 m]

200'
[61.0 m]

150'
[45.7 m]

100'
[30.5 m] 0   50'   100'   150'   200'

SITE ZONING

SITE SECTION
1" = 40' [1:500 METRIC]

SITE PARKING

An existing snack shop with outdoor deck is located next to a lake. On the site plan shown on the following page, you must develop a paved parking area to serve the snack shop according to the following requirements. Assume that the site is nearly level.

1. Draw a paved parking lot that will accommodate a total of 50 spaces. Show each space.

   - 45 standard, 10 ft × 20 ft (3 m × 6.1 m) spaces are required.
   - 5 accessible, 12 ft × 20 ft (3.7 m × 6.1 m) spaces are required.
   - All parking must be perpendicular to the traffic aisles.
   - No parallel parking is permitted.

2. Draw all traffic aisles and drives required to connect the parking to the street with the following requirements:

   - Only one curb cut is permitted.
   - The drives and traffic aisles must be 25 ft (7.6 m) wide.

   - Dead-end parking is not allowed.
   - Drive-through circulation is required.
   - The intersection of the access drive and the street must be perpendicular for at least 25 ft (7.6 m) of the drive.

3. Additional requirements:

   - Paving cannot disturb any existing trees or other site features.
   - Paving cannot be closer than 40 ft (12.2 m) from the building.
   - Paving (except the access drive) cannot be placed within the setback.
   - Paving must be minimized.

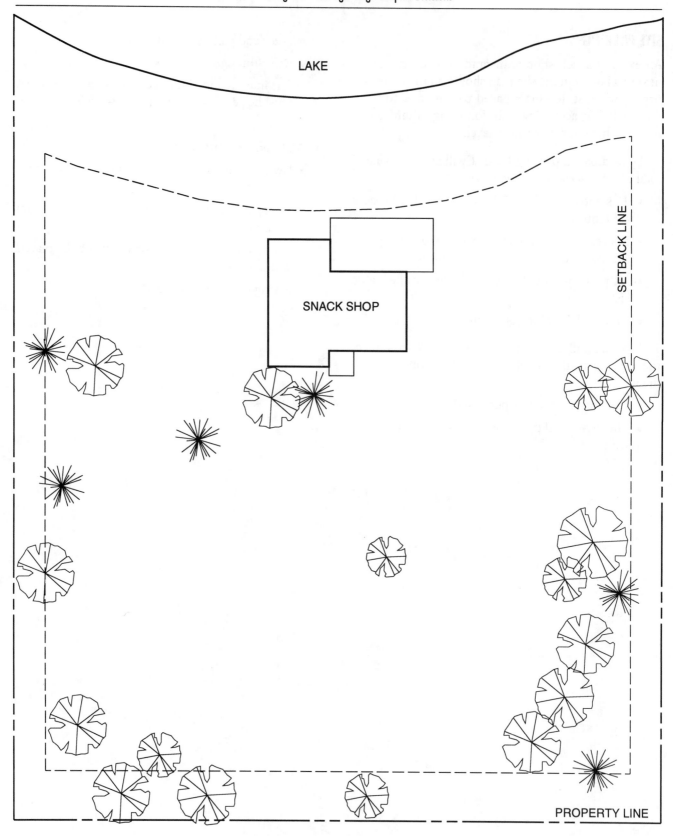

LAKE

SETBACK LINE

SNACK SHOP

PROPERTY LINE

LAKE AVENUE

SITE PLAN

SCALE: 1" = 60' [1:720 METRIC]

SITE PARKING

SITE ANALYSIS

Given the existing site plan shown on the following page, you are required to determine the allowable area for building and other site developments and draw their limits. The regulatory and developmental constraints are as follows.

1. Draw the limits suitable for building, and cross-hatch.

   - Setbacks are measured from the property lines. Construction of buildings is prohibited within these setbacks.
   - Front setback (Howe Avenue) = 40 ft (12.2 m).
   - Rear setback (west property line) = 20 ft (6.1 m).
   - Side yard setbacks = 20 ft (6.1 m).

2. Draw the limits of the area available for parking, and label. Parking may be placed anywhere inside a line 15 ft (4.6 m) from all property lines.

3. Observe the following additional restrictions:

   - Construction of buildings and other surface improvements is prohibited within 30 ft (9.1 m) of the edge of the ditch.
   - There is a use restriction prohibiting the placement of any part of a building within 40 ft (12.2 m) of the south property line.
   - Construction of buildings is prohibited within the utility easement, which is 40 ft (12.2 m) wide.

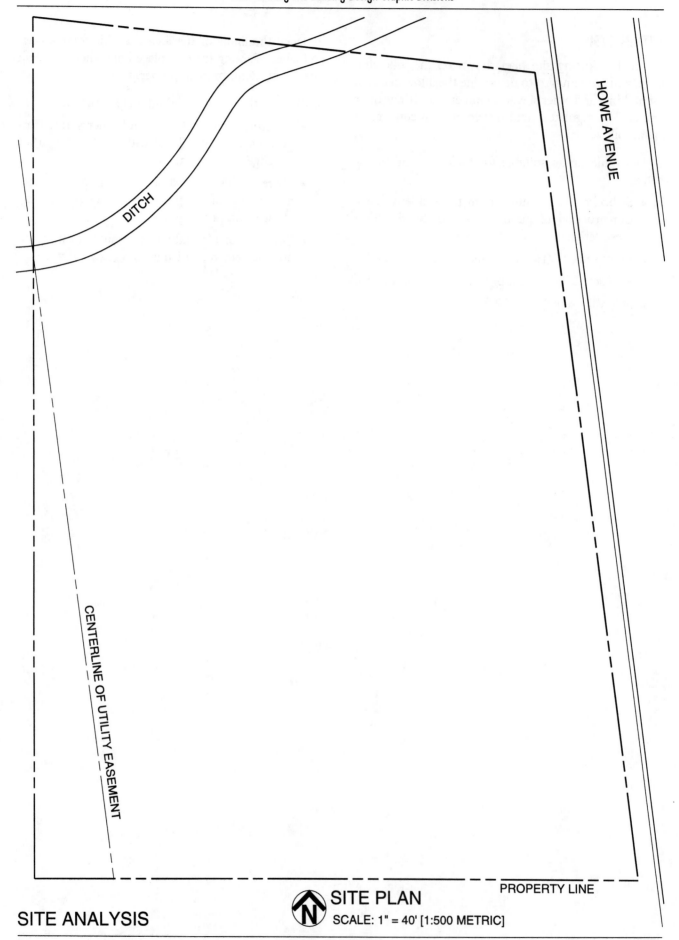

DITCH

CENTERLINE OF UTILITY EASEMENT

HOWE AVENUE

PROPERTY LINE

SITE ANALYSIS

SITE PLAN
SCALE: 1" = 40' [1:500 METRIC]

SITE SECTION

You have been asked to locate a cellular phone satellite office, parking area, and transmission tower on a gently sloping hill. The profile of the hill and the profiles of the facilities are shown on the following page. You must show how the site can be regraded and the facilities located to satisfy the following requirements.

1. Place the office so that both levels are accessible to grade.

- The building setback from the south property line is 100 ft (30.5 m).
- The building and tower setback from the north property line is 20 ft (6.1 m).
- The office cannot be located on fill.
- There must be positive drainage from both sides of the office for a minimum distance of 10 ft (3 m).

2. Place the parking lot so that it is no more than 15 ft (4.6 m) vertically and 30 ft (9.1 m) horizontally from the office.

3. Place the tower so that the top-most portion is at least at elevation 190 ft (57.9 m) but no more than elevation 210 ft (64.0 m).

4. Draw a new grade line so that the minimum slope at a cut or fill is 5:1 (5 units horizontal to 1 vertical) and the maximum slope at a cut or fill is 2:1.

5. You must observe the following additional conditions:

- The grade line at the property lines must match existing grade outside the property.
- No retaining walls are permitted.
- All items must be fully supported by existing or new grade.
- No excavation into bedrock is permitted.

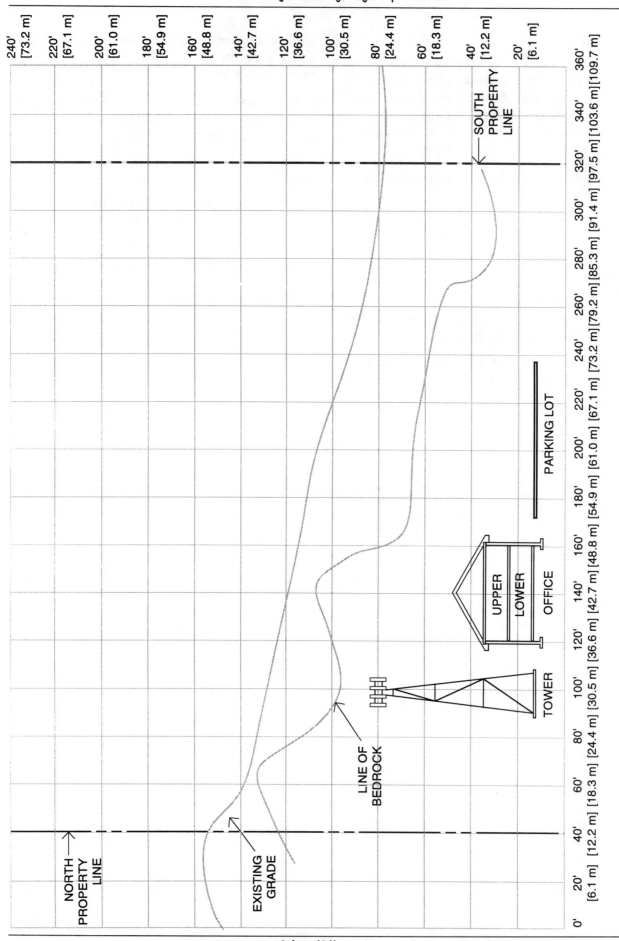

SITE SECTION

SITE SECTION TOWARD THE EAST

SCALE: 1" = 40' [1:500 METRIC]

SITE GRADING

An outdoor dining area is being planned for an existing restaurant located as shown on the following page. The existing site contours and vegetation are also shown. Draw a site plan that satisfies the following requirements.

1. Regrade the site so water will flow around and away from the patio and restaurant.

2. The spot elevations at the corners of the patio shall remain unchanged.

3. The trunks of the two trees are to remain undisturbed.

4. No retaining walls or guardrails are permitted.

5. The grade elevations at the building and along the east side of the site must remain.

6. The slope of the regraded portions of the site shall not exceed 50%.

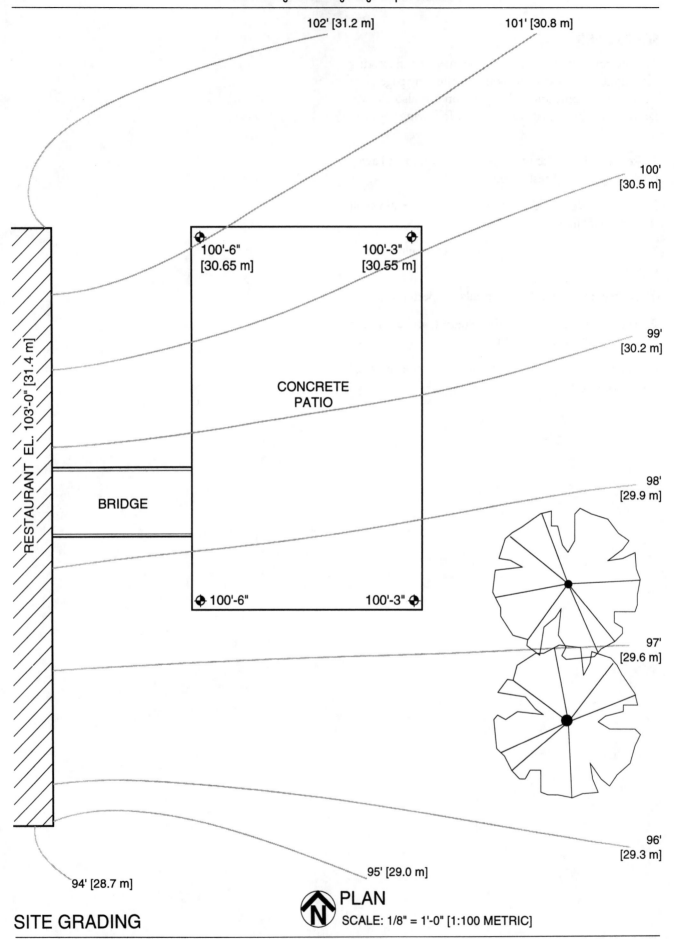

102' [31.2 m]

101' [30.8 m]

100'
[30.5 m]

100'-6"
[30.65 m]

100'-3"
[30.55 m]

99'
[30.2 m]

CONCRETE
PATIO

98'
[29.9 m]

RESTAURANT EL. 103'-0" [31.4 m]

BRIDGE

100'-6"

100'-3"

97'
[29.6 m]

96'
[29.3 m]

95' [29.0 m]

94' [28.7 m]

PLAN
SCALE: 1/8" = 1'-0" [1:100 METRIC]

SITE GRADING

2

Building Planning

BLOCK DIAGRAM

The members of a church have decided to build a small chapel and meeting room to the east of the church's present site and parking area. Prepare a block diagram for the chapel building using the program, the following additional requirements, and the bubble diagram shown.

1. The entry lobby must face the parking area. Do not show pedestrian circulation.

2. A second exit is required from the building through the hallway.

3. The chapel must be rectangular in shape with access from one long side of the room to the drop-off area to the east.

4. The chapel must have direct access from the lobby.

5. Dead-end corridors shall not exceed 20 ft (6.1 m).

6. The activity room must be directly adjacent to the chapel to allow for a movable partition between the rooms.

7. The site is flat. The building is limited to one story in height.

8. The building must fit within the building limit lines and be oriented to relate to the site context without disturbing any existing conditions.

Block Diagram Program

Abbreviation	Spaces	ft²	m²
CH	chapel	1800	167
AC	main activity room	900	84
EL	entrance lobby	500	46
RO	robing room	150	14
OF	office	300	28
ST	storage	200	19
RR	restrooms	400	37
ME	mechanical	400	37
H	hall	250	23
	TOTAL	4900	455

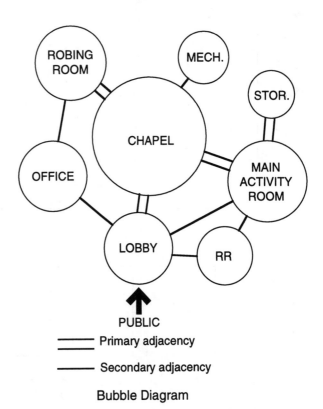

Bubble Diagram

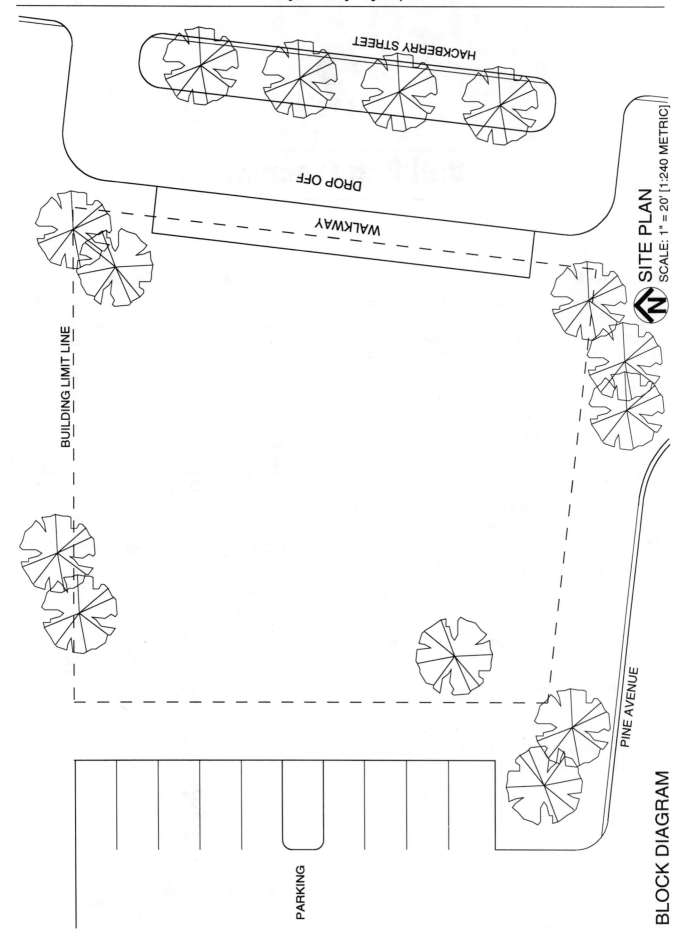

HACKBERRY STREET

DROP OFF

WALKWAY

BUILDING LIMIT LINE

SITE PLAN
SCALE: 1" = 20' [1:240 METRIC]

PINE AVENUE

PARKING

BLOCK DIAGRAM

INTERIOR LAYOUT

A small management company has leased space in an existing building. The space is approximately 1470 ft² (137 m²) with three windows as shown on the floor plan on the following page. You are required to develop a space plan and furniture layout that meets the program and code requirements listed here.

1. All spaces and workstations must comply with the accessibility requirements given in the code below (including the clear space for a wheelchair to make a 180° turn).

2. The furniture layout must allow for reasonable clearances and access to all of the furniture elements. You must place all the furniture listed in the Space and Furniture Requirements.

3. All spaces, including the reception space, must be labeled. (On the computer test there is a specific label that must be used.)

4. The furniture to be placed is shown in the diagram on the following page.

Space and Furniture Requirements

1. Reception Area (RA)
    1 secretarial desk with chair
    4 lounge chairs
    1 round coffee table
    1 large bookcase
    1 display rack

2. Manager's Office (MO)
    1 executive desk with chair
    1 credenza
    2 side chairs
    2 lateral files
    1 large bookcase

3. Agents' Offices (AO)—two agent offices are required
    1 executive desk
    1 credenza
    2 side chairs
    1 small bookcase
    1 lateral file

4. Conference Room (CR)
    1 conference table with chairs
    1 credenza

5. Workroom (WR)
    1 copy machine
    1 work table
    3 lateral files

Interior Layout Code Requirements

1. The space required for a wheelchair to make a 180° turn is a clear space of 60 in. (1525 mm) diameter.

2. The minimum clear distance between walls or between a wall and any other obstruction along an aisle or corridor shall be 36 in. (914 mm).

3. Doorways must have a clear opening of 32 in. (813 mm) when the door is open 90 degrees, measured between the face of the door and the opposite stop.

4. Minimum maneuvering clearances at doors shall be as shown on the accompanying illustration.

5. If doorways have two independently operated door leaves, then at least one leaf shall meet the preceding requirements for clear width and maneuvering clearances.

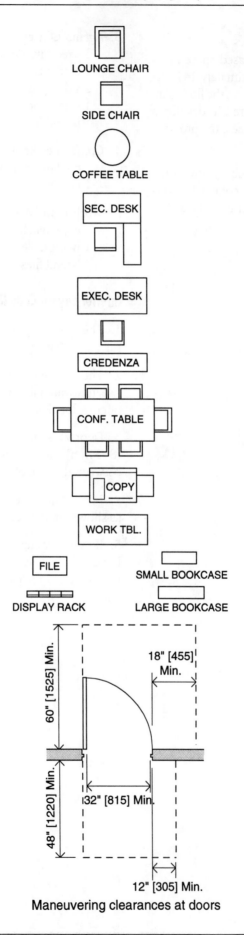

LOUNGE CHAIR

SIDE CHAIR

COFFEE TABLE

SEC. DESK

EXEC. DESK

CREDENZA

CONF. TABLE

COPY

WORK TBL.

FILE

DISPLAY RACK

SMALL BOOKCASE

LARGE BOOKCASE

60" [1525] Min.

18" [455] Min.

48" [1220] Min.

32" [815] Min.

12" [305] Min.

Maneuvering clearances at doors

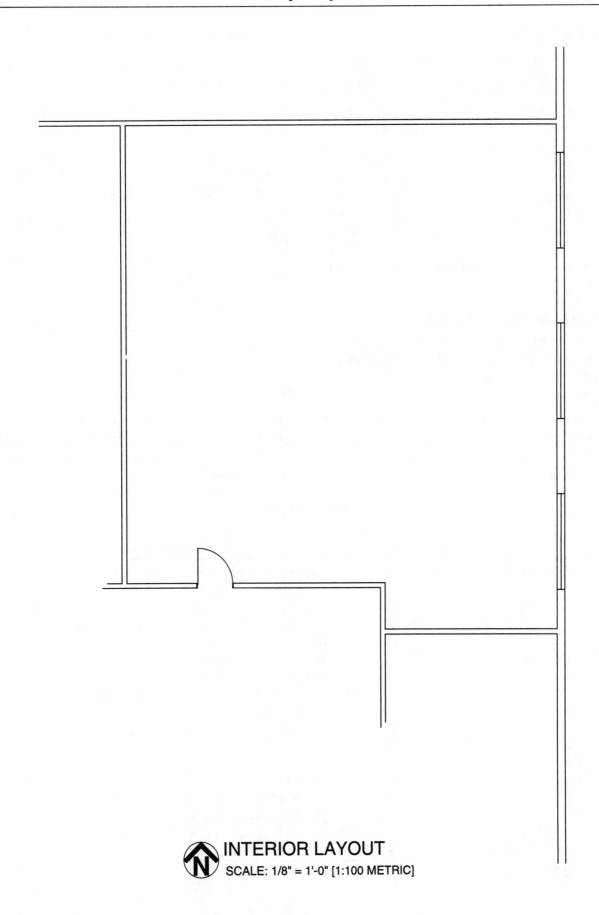

INTERIOR LAYOUT
SCALE: 1/8" = 1'-0" [1:100 METRIC]

SCHEMATIC DESIGN

You have been asked to provide a schematic design for a small two-story building. You must develop both first- and second-level floor plans on the site plan shown on the following page. The schematic design must be responsive to the given program and code requirements and should reflect principles of sound design logic. The orientation of the building on the site must be responsive to site influences. You must indicate partition locations, corridors as required, doors, windows, and the location of the upper story of the two-story space. (On the computer test you must use the included label to indicate this space on the second-floor plan.) Label each space with the tag abbreviation included in the space program.

Schematic Design Vignette Program

A midwestern city is constructing a neighborhood community center. The center will be used primarily as a meeting site and for organized activities for children, teens, and seniors.

1. The center is in a residential area adjacent to a small park to the north of the site. Parking is across the street to the east, so the main entrance must be on the east portion of the site.

2. The major views are to the north and south.

3. The kitchen must have access to service from the alley on the west and have direct access to the corridor.

4. The kitchen must be adjacent to the main activity room.

5. The main activity room must have a finished ceiling height of 14 ft (4.3 m). All other spaces shall have a 9 ft (2.7 m) finished ceiling height.

6. The meeting room on the second floor must be capable of being divided into two smaller rooms with a movable partition; when partitioned, each subdivided room must have a separate entrance.

7. Egress may be in any direction.

8. The area of each space shall be within 10% of the required program area.

9. The total corridor area shall not exceed 25% of the total program area.

10. The second-floor envelope must be congruent with or wholly contained within the first-floor envelope, except that doors to the exterior may be recessed for weather protection.

Spaces Program

Tag	Name	Area (ft²)	Area (m²)	Requirements
RL	reception/lobby	400	40	Main entrance connects to reception/lobby. Exterior window required.
MA	main activity room	1000	100	Exterior windows required.
SA	senior activities room	600	60	Adjacent to reception area. Exterior window required.
K	kitchen	300	30	Immediately adjacent to main activity room.
AS	activity storage	100	10	Must open onto main activity room.
T	toilet rooms	800	80	two per floor @ 200 ft² (20 m²) each.
ST	stairs	640	64	two per floor @ 160 ft² (16 m²) per stair.
E	elevator shaft	140	14	one per floor @ 70 ft² (7 m²). Min. dimension 7 ft (2.1 m).
EE	elevator equipment	70	7	Adjacent to elevator shaft.
EM	electrical/mechanical	300	30	
J	janitor's closet, first floor	50	5	
C	coats	50	5	Adjacent to lobby.
O	offices	600	60	four @ 150 ft² (15 m²) on second floor. Exterior windows required.
MR	meeting room	600	60	Second floor. Exterior window required.
J	janitor's closet, second floor	30	3	
	TOTAL PROGRAM AREA	5680	568	

Schematic Design Vignette Code

Comply with the following code requirements. These are the *only* code-related criteria you are required to use.

Exiting Requirements

1. Two exits are required from each floor separated by at least one-half the maximum overall diagonal distance of the floor.

2. Two exits are required in the main activity room and senior activity room. They must be separated by a minimum of one-half the maximum overall diagonal distance of the room. Exit doors may discharge directly to the exterior of the building at grade.

3. Every room must connect directly to a corridor or circulation area. Exceptions: elevator equipment rooms, activity storage, and rooms with an area of 50 ft² (5 m²) or less may connect to a corridor or circulation area through an intervening space.

4. Exit doors must swing in the direction of travel.

5. Door swings cannot reduce the minimum clear exit path to less than 44 in. (1118 mm).

Corridors

1. Discharge corridors directly to the exterior at grade or through stairs or circulation areas.

2. The minimum width of corridors is 6 ft (1830 mm).

3. The maximum dead-end corridor length is 20 ft (6100 mm).

4. Do not interrupt corridors with intervening rooms. Circulation areas are not considered to be intervening rooms.

Stairs

1. Discharge stairs directly to the exterior at grade.

2. The minimum width of stairs is 4 ft (1220 mm).

3. Connect stairs directly to a corridor or circulation area at each floor.

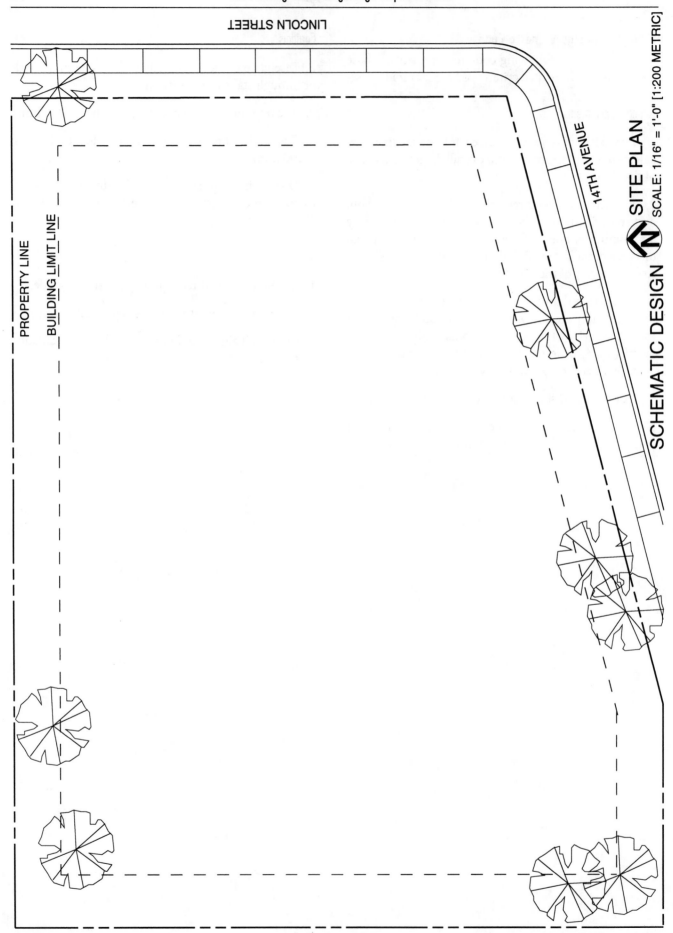

LINCOLN STREET

14TH AVENUE

PROPERTY LINE

BUILDING LIMIT LINE

SITE PLAN

SCALE: 1/16" = 1'-0" [1:200 METRIC]

SCHEMATIC DESIGN

3

Building Technology

BUILDING SECTION

For this vignette you must draw a building section corresponding to the section cut line on the plans for a two-story building. You must draw the exterior walls, foundation, interior partitions, finished ceilings, structural elements, HVAC equipment, and anything else that is cut by the cut line as well as joists in elevation immediately adjacent to the cut line. The section must accurately reflect the dimensions and spatial relations given in the program and on the plans. Vertical spacing not explicitly stated in the program must be accurately interpreted and indicated on the section.

Building Section Program

The structural system for this vignette consists of top-chord bearing steel joists on masonry bearing walls with spread footings and a concrete slab on grade.

1. All ceilings and roofs are flat with a 4 in. (100 mm) concrete slab on the joists.

2. The ceiling height of the lounge is 17'-0" (5180 mm). The ceiling height of the other first- and second-floor spaces is 8'-6" (2590 mm).

3. The space between each ceiling and floor or roof slab must be held to the minimum dimension required to accommodate light fixtures and the mechanical and structural components shown on the plans.

4. All ducts must be placed below the joists.

5. Provide 12 in. (305 mm) of clearance between the bottom of the ducts and the finished ceiling to accommodate light fixtures and sprinkler pipe.

6. Ceiling spaces must be used as return air plenums.

7. The frost depth is 3'-6" (1067 mm) below grade.

8. Parapets must extend 2'-6" (760 mm) above the surface of decks at roof edges and at changes in the roof deck elevation.

9. Corridor walls must have a one-hour fire-resistive rating.

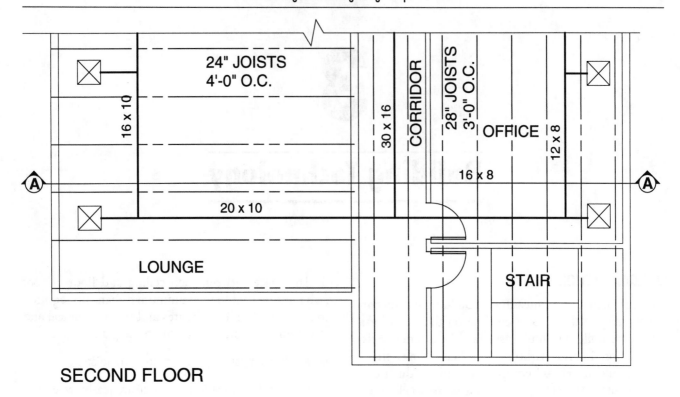

SECOND FLOOR

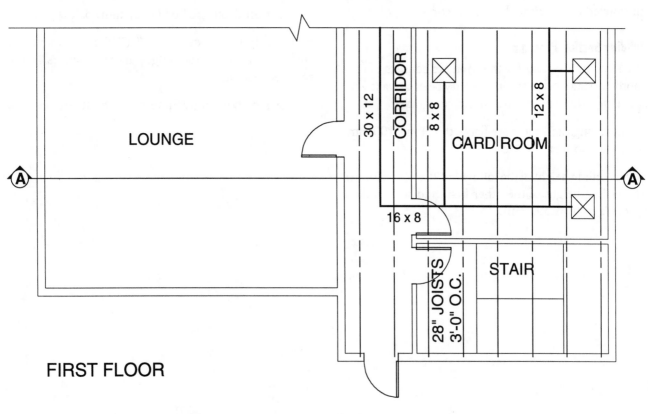

FIRST FLOOR

BUILDING SECTION
1/8" = 1'-0" [1:100 METRIC]

STRUCTURAL LAYOUT

For this vignette you must create a structural framing solution for a small two-story building based on a given floor plan and program requirements. The layout must include the designation of bearing walls where existing walls are shown, columns, beams, and roof joists. All walls are assumed to be non-load-bearing unless you designate them otherwise with the tool provided. Decking must also be shown with an arrow indicating the direction of the decking.

Structural Vignette Program

You are required to develop a roof framing layout of a small truck service company. The layout must accommodate the requirements given here.

Site/Foundation

1. The soils and foundation system are adequate for all normal loads.

2. There are no wind or seismic loading requirements.

3. Concentrated or special loads need not be considered.

Materials

1. The structural system shall consist of open-web steel joists on structural steel or bearing walls.

2. The metal deck on the joists is capable of carrying loads on spans up to and including 4'-0" (1200 mm).

General Requirements

1. The roof over the service bays is 16 ft (4880 mm) above the floor. The roof over the remaining spaces is 12 ft (3660 mm) above the floor.

2. All roof framing is flat.

3. The service bay area must be column free.

4. Columns may be located within walls, including the clerestory window wall.

5. Any wall shown on the floor plan may be designated a bearing wall. Additional bearing walls are not allowed.

6. The glazed opening between the office area and the service bays must remain column free.

7. The structure must accommodate a clerestory window along the full length of the east wall of the service bay area.

8. No cantilevers are allowed.

9. Lintels must be shown at all openings in bearing walls.

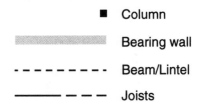

Structural Vignette Legend

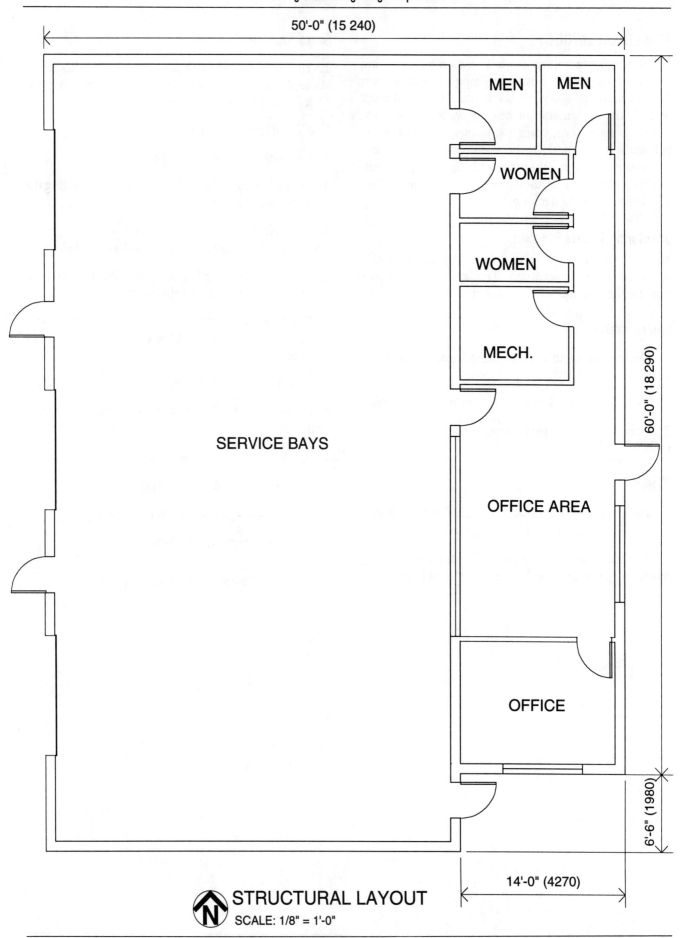

50'-0" (15 240)

MEN   MEN

WOMEN

WOMEN

MECH.

SERVICE BAYS

60'-0" (18 290)

OFFICE AREA

OFFICE

6'-6" (1980)

14'-0" (4270)

STRUCTURAL LAYOUT
SCALE: 1/8" = 1'-0"

ACCESSIBILITY—RAMP

You have been asked to develop a stair and ramp system and doorway to connect the lower level of an entry lobby to a slightly raised portion of a building as shown on the accompanying floor plan. You must indicate all ramps, stairs, railings, walls, doors, and landings required to complete the plan in conformance to the program and code requirements and to principles of design logic.

Accessibility—Ramp Program

1. Provide an accessible circulation system including a ramp and stairway to connect the lower level of the lobby with the exit corridor level.

2. Locate a wall and door on the upper level to separate the lobby from the exit corridor.

3. No portion of the ramp or stairs may encroach on the existing upper level.

4. Show the elevation of all new landings.

Accessibility—Ramp Code Requirements

General

1. The minimum width of an exit route shall not be less than 44 in. (1120 mm).

2. Projections into a required exit route width are prohibited, except for handrail projections.

3. The space required for a wheelchair to make a 180° turn is a clear space of 60 in. (1525 mm) diameter.

Stairs

1. The minimum width shall not be less than 44 in. (1120 mm).

2. Projections into a required stairway are prohibited, except for handrail projections.

3. The minimum dimension measured in the direction of travel shall not be less than the width of the stairway.

4. On any given flight of stairs, all steps shall have uniform riser heights and uniform tread widths. Stair treads shall be no less than 11 in. (280 mm) wide, measured from riser to riser. Stair risers shall be no more than 7 in. (180 mm) and no less than 4 in. (100 mm).

Ramps

1. Any part of an accessible route with a slope greater than 1:20 shall be considered a ramp and shall comply with the three following requirements.

2. The maximum slope of a ramp in new construction shall be 1:12. The maximum rise for any run shall be 30 in. (760 mm).

3. The minimum clear width of a ramp shall be 44 in. (915 mm). Projections into a required ramp width are prohibited, except for handrail projections.

4. Ramps shall have level landings at the bottom and top of each ramp run, at all points of turning, and at doors. Landings shall have the following features:

- The landing shall be at least as wide as the ramp run leading to it.
- The minimum dimension in the direction of travel shall be 60 in. (1525 mm).
- If ramps change direction at landings, the minimum dimension shall be 60 in. (1525 mm).
- If a doorway is located at a landing, then the area in front of the doorway shall have maneuvering clearances as described in the code section on doors.

Handrails

1. Stairways and ramps shall have handrails on both sides. Exception: handrails are not required on ramps where the vertical rise between landings is 6 in. (150 mm) or less.

2. Handrails shall be continuous within the full length of each ramp run or stair flight. The inside handrail on switchback or dogleg stairs and ramps shall be continuous.

3. If ramp handrails are not continuous, they shall extend at least 12 in. (305 mm) beyond the top and bottom of the ramp segment and shall be parallel with the floor or ground surface.

4. If stair handrails are not continuous, they shall extend at least 12 in. (305 mm) beyond the top and bottom risers.

5. Stairways more than 88 in. (2235 mm) wide shall have intermediate handrails.

Guardrails

Open sides of landings, floor surfaces, ramps, and stairways shall be protected by a continuous guardrail.

Doors

1. Doorways shall have a minimum clear opening of 32 in. (815 mm) with the door open 90 degrees, measured between the face of the door and the opposite stop.

2. Exit doors shall swing in the direction of egress travel.

3. Minimum maneuvering clearances at doors shall be as shown in the following illustration.

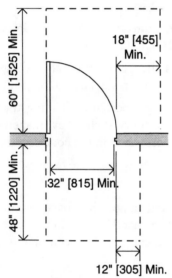

Maneuvering clearances at doors

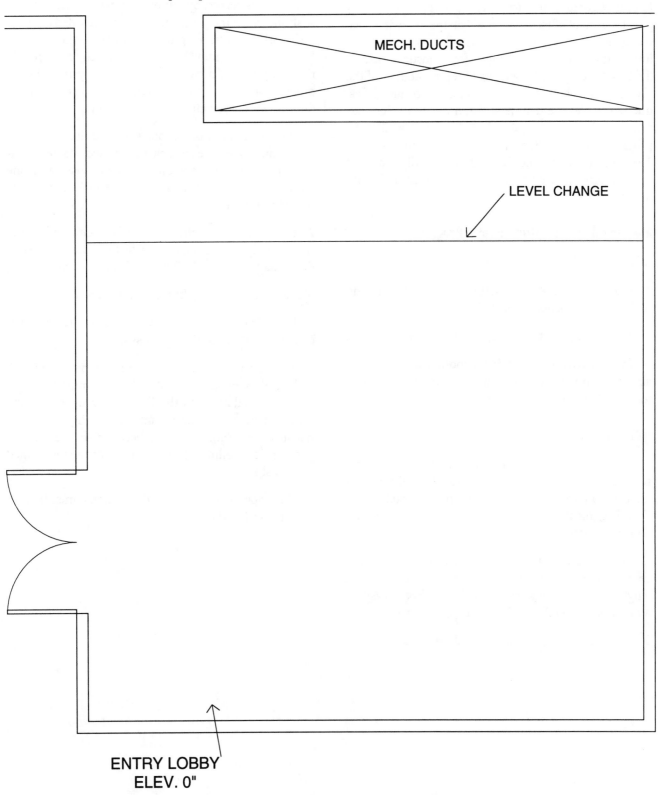

EXIT CORRIDOR
ELEV. 26" [660]

MECH. DUCTS

LEVEL CHANGE

ENTRY LOBBY
ELEV. 0"

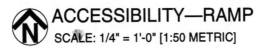

ACCESSIBILITY—RAMP
SCALE: 1/4" = 1'-0" [1:50 METRIC]

MECHANICAL AND ELECTRICAL PLAN

For this vignette you must complete the reflected ceiling plan for a small office suite shown on the following page using the symbols shown below the floor plan. Your solution must show a ceiling grid for acoustical tile and lighting fixtures, and a schematic representation of the HVAC plan including air diffusers, return air grilles, ductwork, and fire dampers. You must locate light fixtures to achieve the required light level indicated in the program using the light distribution diagrams shown. The lighting layout should minimize overlighting and underlighting and provide for maximum flexibility for furniture layouts.

Mechanical and Electrical Vignette Program

Ceiling System

1. Provide a 2 ft × 4 ft (600 mm × 1200 mm) grid with lay-in acoustical tiles in all spaces.

2. The ceiling height in all spaces is 9'-0" (2740 mm).

3. Interior partitions terminate about 4 in. (100 mm) above the finished ceiling. Fire-rated partitions extend to the bottom of the floor deck above.

Lighting System

1. For all spaces except the reception area, use only recessed fluorescent fixtures to provide uniform light distribution with a light level of approximately 70 fc (700 lux) measured at approximately 2'-6" (760 mm) above the floor.

2. For the reception area, use only recessed incandescent fixtures to provide uniform light distribution with a light level of approximately 70 fc (700 lux) measured at approximately 2'-0" (610 mm) above the floor.

3. Provide for efficient, uniform illumination.

HVAC System

The space is served by supply and return risers in the shaft shown on the plan. Supply air is provided through ductwork. Return air grilles are open to the plenum. However, the plenum must be connected to the return riser with rigid ductwork. The HVAC system should provide for uniform air distribution with an economical duct layout conforming to the following.

1. Provide a minimum of one supply diffuser and one return air grille in each space. An acceptable distribution pattern includes one supply diffuser and one return air grille for every 150 ft^2. (14 m^2) of floor area or fraction thereof.

2. Each supply air diffuser must be connected to the rigid supply duct system with flexible duct. Flexible ducts may not exceed 10 ft (3050 mm) in length.

3. Flexible ducts may fit through joist webs.

4. Each air diffuser must have a separate flexible duct connecting it to the rigid duct system.

5. Rigid ducts fit under beams, in spaces between joists, and in a zone that extends 2 ft (600 mm) from the beams and adjacent to the fire-rated walls separating the space from adjacent tenant spaces. Rigid ducts do not fit through joist webs or between the bottoms of joists and the ceiling except for the 2 ft zone mentioned previously.

6. Duct openings in fire-rated partitions must be protected with fire dampers.

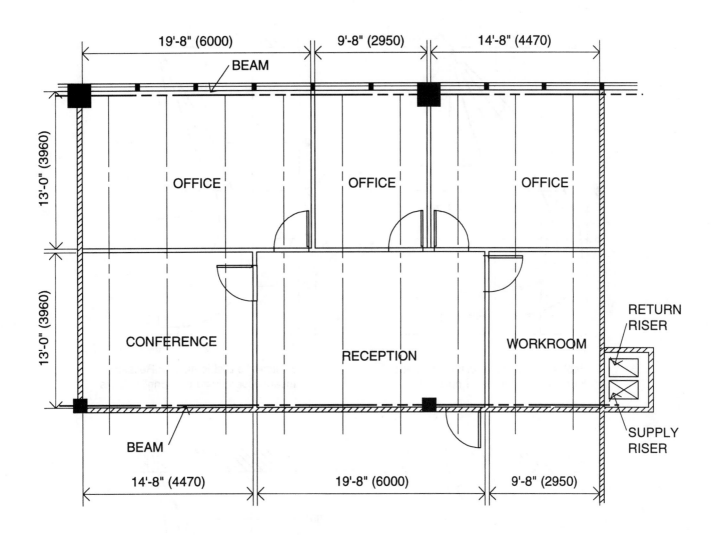

19'-8" (6000)   9'-8" (2950)   14'-8" (4470)

BEAM

13'-0" (3960)

OFFICE   OFFICE   OFFICE

13'-0" (3960)

CONFERENCE   RECEPTION   WORKROOM

BEAM

RETURN RISER

SUPPLY RISER

14'-8" (4470)   19'-8" (6000)   9'-8" (2950)

⊠	Recessed fluorescent fixture
O	Recessed incandescent fixture
⊠	Supply air diffuser
⊠	Return air grille
—	Rigid supply duct
- - - - -	Flexible supply duct
//////	Fire-rated wall
—·—·—	Bar joist
◤	Fire damper

MECHANICAL AND ELECTRICAL PLAN
SCALE: 1/8" = 1'-0" [1:100 metric]

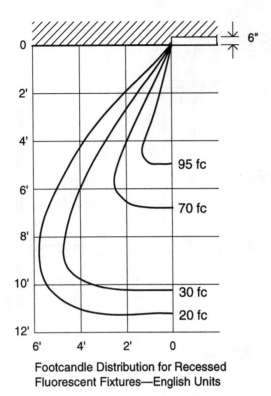

Footcandle Distribution for Recessed
Fluorescent Fixtures—English Units

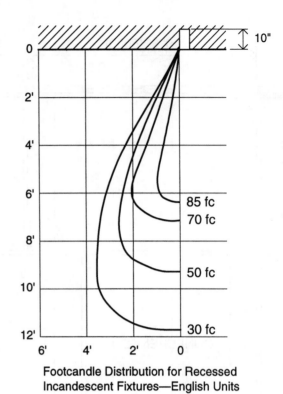

Footcandle Distribution for Recessed
Incandescent Fixtures—English Units

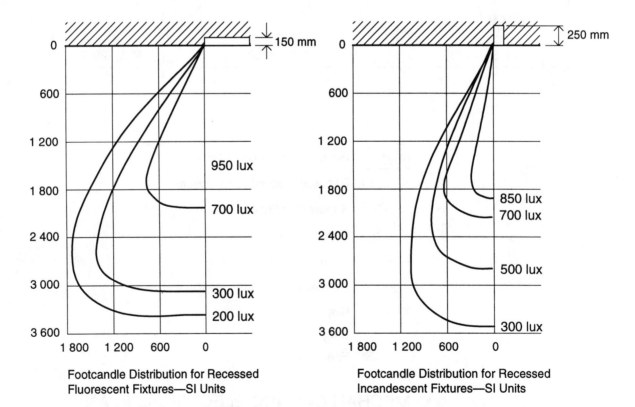

Footcandle Distribution for Recessed
Fluorescent Fixtures—SI Units

Footcandle Distribution for Recessed
Incandescent Fixtures—SI Units

LIGHTING DIAGRAMS

STAIR DESIGN

You have been asked to design an exit stairway for an existing two-story building with a maintenance office located at a third level slightly above the first floor as shown in the section drawing. The base floor plans are shown on the following page. Your design must provide a means of egress from the second floor and from the maintenance office to the door leading to the public way on the first floor. On the floor plans provided, draw the stairway, including all required handrails and guardrails. Indicate the elevations of all stair flights, at the top of the highest tread and at the bottom of the lowest riser, to match adjacent landing elevations.

The total occupant load and the number of exits for each level of the building are as follows.

Building Level	Total Occupant Load	No. of Exits
first floor	340	2
maintenance office	3	1
second floor	340	2

The stairway must provide a means of egress from all three levels and must provide a continuous path from the second floor to the first floor exit. The stairs will be constructed of precast concrete components that have landings 12 in. (305 mm) thick and stair flights 12 in. (305 mm) thick measured from the stair nosing to the soffit below.

Your design must comply with the following code requirements.

Stair Design Vignette Code Requirements

Capacity of Exit Components

1. The occupant load for each exit shall be determined by dividing the total occupant load for an individual floor by the number of exits serving that floor.

2. Where stairways serve more than one level, the capacity of the exit components shall be based on the individual floor with the largest occupant load, provided that the exit capacity shall not decrease in the direction of the means of egress.

3. The width of each exit component in inches shall be not less than the occupant load served by an exit multiplied by 0.3, nor less than the minimum width specified by this code.

Stairways

1. The minimum width shall be computed in accordance with the preceding requirement for Capacity of Exit Components, but shall not be less than 44 in. (1120 mm).

2. Projections into a required stairway are prohibited, except for handrail projections.

3. The minimum dimension of landings shall not be less than the required width of the stairs.

4. On any given flight of stairs, all steps shall have uniform riser heights and uniform tread depths. Stair treads shall be no less than 11 in. (280 mm) deep measured from riser to riser. Stair risers shall be no more than 7 in. (180 mm) and no less than 4 in. (100 mm).

5. The minimum headroom of all parts of a stairway shall not be less than 80 in. (2030 mm) measured vertically from the tread nosing or from any floor surface, including landings.

Handrails

1. Stairways shall have handrails on both sides.

2. Handrails shall be continuous within the full length of each stair flight. The inside handrail on switchback or dogleg stairs shall be continuous.

3. If stair handrails are not continuous, at least one handrail shall extend at least 12 in. (305 mm) beyond the top and bottom risers.

4. Stairways more than 88 in. (2235 mm) wide shall have intermediate handrails.

Guardrails

Open sides of landings, floor surfaces, and stairways shall be protected by a continuous guardrail.

Doors

1. When opening, doors shall not reduce the width of landings to less than one-half of the required width.

2. There shall be a floor or landing on each side of a door and the floor surface on both sides of the door shall be at the same elevation.

Area of Refuge

1. An accessible area of refuge serving the second floor shall be provided within the stair enclosure.

2. The area of refuge shall be sized to accommodate one wheelchair space of 30 in. × 48 in. (760 mm × 1220 mm) for each 150 occupants or portion thereof, based on the stairway occupant load. Such spaces shall not reduce the required stair or landing width.

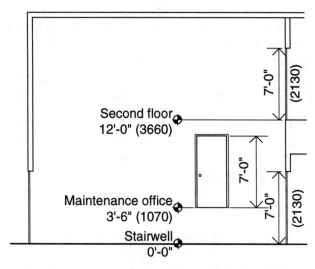

SECTION A-A

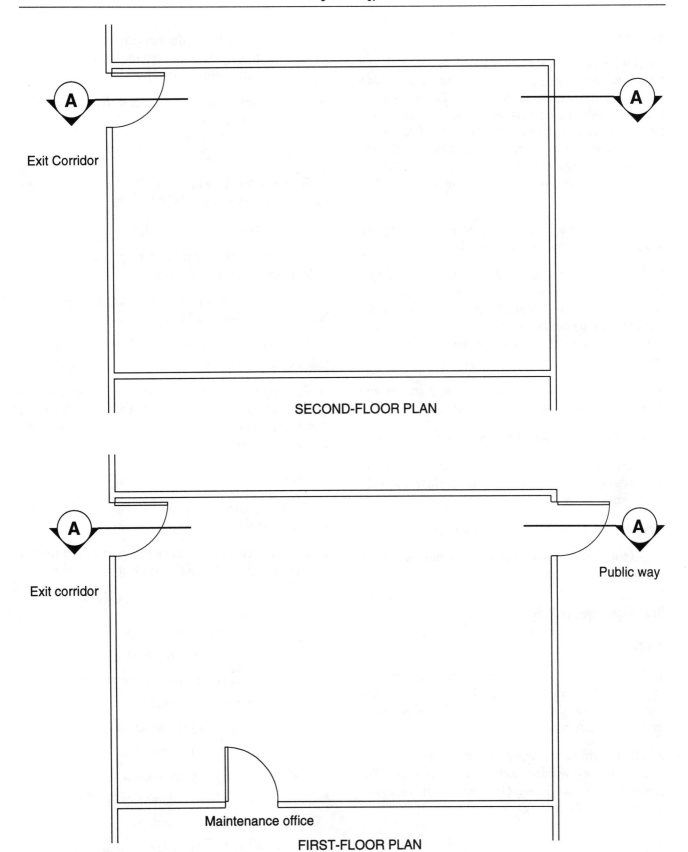

Exit Corridor

SECOND-FLOOR PLAN

Exit corridor

Public way

Maintenance office

FIRST-FLOOR PLAN

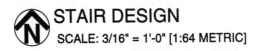 STAIR DESIGN

SCALE: 3/16" = 1'-0" [1:64 METRIC]

ROOF PLAN

The roof system of a small visitors' center is shown on the following page. The outermost edges of two roofs are indicated by dashed lines. The higher roof is over the information/display area and the lower roof covers the remainder of the building. Configure these roofs for the effective removal of rainwater, satisfying the following requirements and the Roof Plan Vignette Program. Use the symbols shown in the Roof Plan Legend.

1. Confine your solution to the areas defined by the dashed lines. Do not use eaves or overhangs.

2. For each roof area, define the extent, slope, and spot elevations of a plane or planes designed to remove rainwater using only roof slope, gutter, and downspouts. The outside edges of the roof planes must coincide with the dashed lines indicating the outermost edges of the roofs.

3. Indicate the location of all necessary gutters and downspouts using the appropriate symbols.

4. Indicate the location of the clerestory.

5. Locate on the roof the HVAC condensing unit and any necessary plumbing vent stacks, skylights, and exhaust fans.

6. Show any necessary flashing and crickets.

7. Set top of roof elevation at the low points of the roof and indicate roof slopes.

Roof Plan Vignette Program

General

1. The building consists of one volume over the information/display area, which must have a high roof, and one volume over the remainder of the building, which must have a low roof.

2. The information/display area must have a continuous clerestory window along the north side. The clerestory is to be 30 in. (760 mm) high, including the head and sill framing.

Roof Drainage

1. Only roof slope, gutters, and downspouts are to be used for removal of rainwater.

2. Rainwater should not discharge from the edge of an upper roof directly onto a lower roof or from any roof or gutter directly onto the ground.

3. Downspouts should not conflict with any door, window, or clerestory.

Construction

1. Finished floor elevation is 0'-0". Ceiling height under the lower roof is 8'-0" (2440 mm).

2. All roof areas must have a slope.

3. The roof over the information/display area shall have a slope between 6:12 and 10:12.

4. The roof over the remainder of the building must have a slope between 3:12 and 5:12.

5. The roof and structural assembly for both roofs is a total of 18 in. (460 mm).

6. Flashing must be provided at all roof/wall intersections. HVAC condensing units, plumbing vent stacks, and exhaust fans are self-flashing and require no additional flashing or crickets.

Mechanical

1. The HVAC condensing unit must be placed on a roof with a slope of 5:12 or less.

2. Place the HVAC condensing unit over a corridor and not closer than 5'-0" (1525 mm) from the roof edge.

3. Provide one exhaust fan for each toilet room.

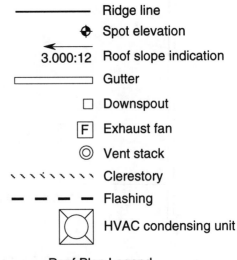

Roof Plan Legend

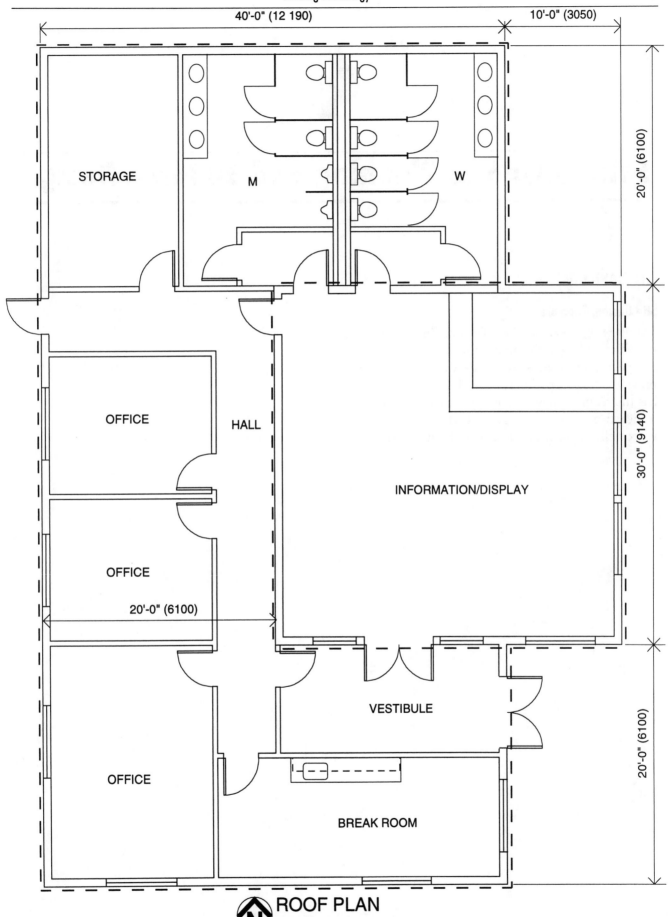

40'-0" (12 190)   10'-0" (3050)

20'-0" (6100)

STORAGE   M   W

30'-0" (9140)

OFFICE   HALL

INFORMATION/DISPLAY

OFFICE

20'-0" (6100)

OFFICE   VESTIBULE

20'-0" (6100)

BREAK ROOM

ROOF PLAN
SCALE: 1/8" = 1'-0" [1:100 metric]

4

Solutions: Site Planning and Building Design

SITE PLANNING

Site Design, Example 1

This is a very good solution. The buildings have been placed according to the program, and the parking area has been positioned to serve the video store and to provide accessible parking for both buildings. The deck has the required view of the wetlands and is shielded by new trees. Both pedestrian and vehicular circulation work well, and only four trees have been disturbed.

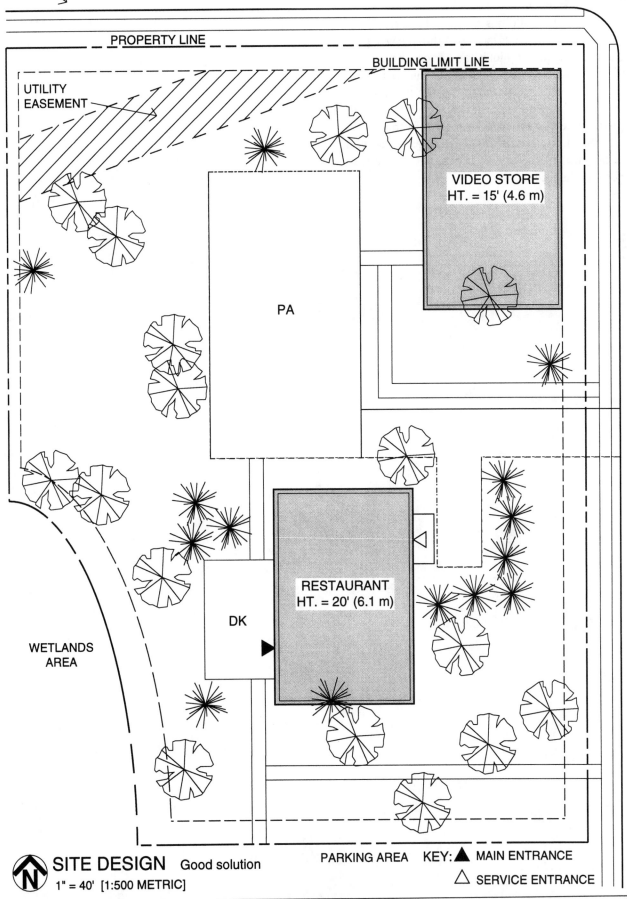

WINDS

STUART STREET

PROPERTY LINE

BUILDING LIMIT LINE

UTILITY EASEMENT

VIDEO STORE
HT. = 15' (4.6 m)

PA

5TH AVENUE

RESTAURANT
HT. = 20' (6.1 m)

DK

WETLANDS AREA

SITE DESIGN Good solution
1" = 40' [1:500 METRIC]

PARKING AREA KEY: ▲ MAIN ENTRANCE
△ SERVICE ENTRANCE

N

Site Design, Example 2

In this solution the buildings are placed appropriately except that the restaurant is located within the wetlands setback area. The parking lot is too narrow and there is no pedestrian access from the street to the restaurant. The curb cut for the driveway is located too close to the corner of the property. Also, six trees have been disturbed. Note that when any program in the A.R.E. calls for trees not to be disturbed, this means that you should not disturb the tree anywhere within the drip line, not just the tree trunk.

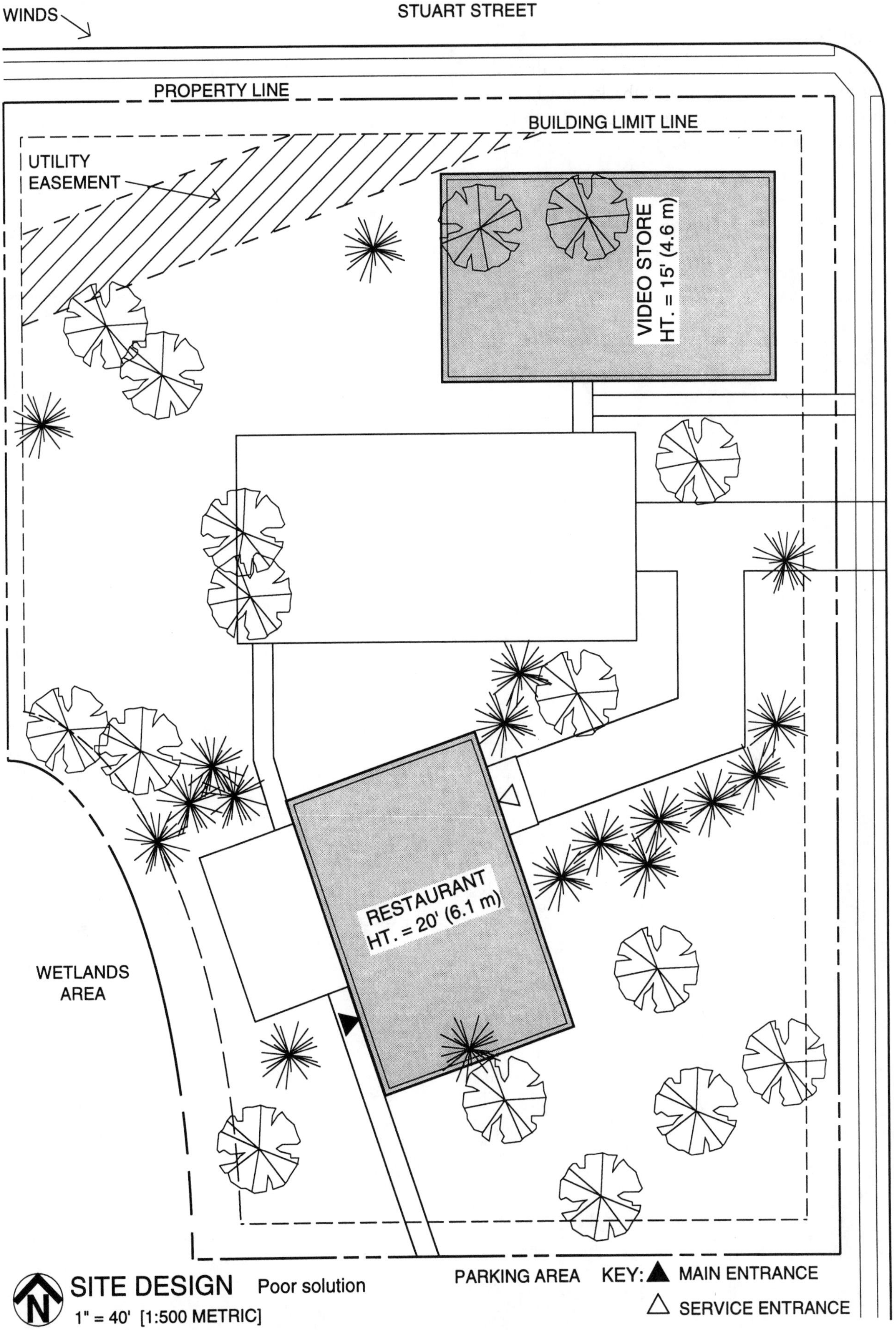

WINDS

STUART STREET

PROPERTY LINE

BUILDING LIMIT LINE

UTILITY
EASEMENT

VIDEO STORE
HT. = 15' (4.6 m)

5TH AVENUE

RESTAURANT
HT. = 20' (6.1 m)

WETLANDS
AREA

SITE DESIGN Poor solution

N

1" = 40' [1:500 METRIC]

PARKING AREA   KEY: ▲ MAIN ENTRANCE

△ SERVICE ENTRANCE

Site Zoning, Example 1

This solution shows the correct grade line profile and
correctly maintains the required setbacks and height
restrictions. The solar access line also begins with the
correct starting point.

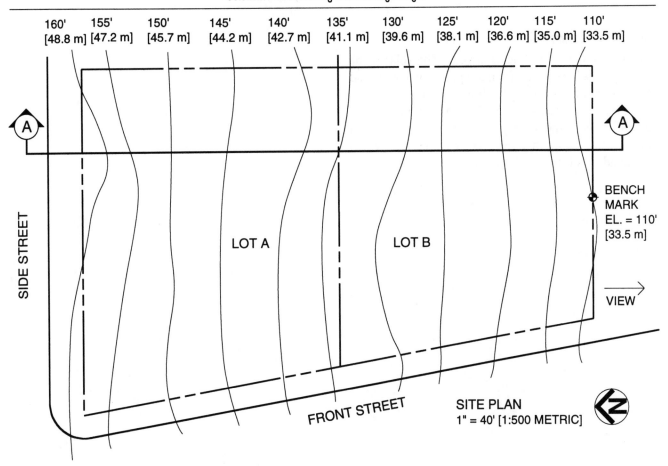

| 160'
[48.8 m] | 155'
[47.2 m] | 150'
[45.7 m] | 145'
[44.2 m] | 140'
[42.7 m] | 135'
[41.1 m] | 130'
[39.6 m] | 125'
[38.1 m] | 120'
[36.6 m] | 115'
[35.0 m] | 110'
[33.5 m] |

SIDE STREET

LOT A   LOT B

BENCH MARK
EL. = 110'
[33.5 m]

VIEW

FRONT STREET

SITE PLAN
1" = 40' [1:500 METRIC]

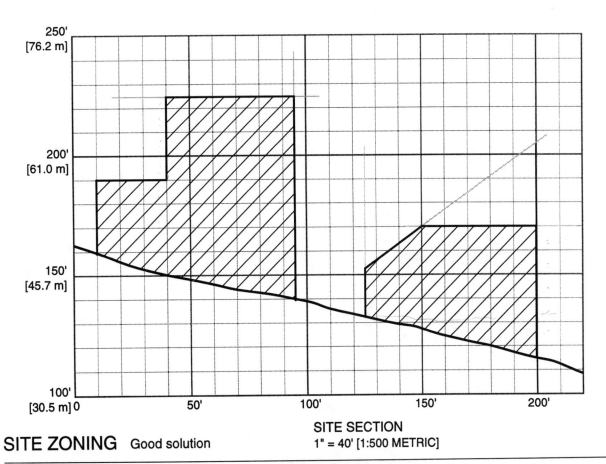

SITE ZONING Good solution

SITE SECTION
1" = 40' [1:500 METRIC]

Site Zoning, Example 2

The solution has two major errors. The solar plane envelope has been taken from the property line instead of the buildings, resulting in a building envelope that is larger than allowed. Also, the 75 ft maximum building height has been incorrectly established from the south building line rather than the average grade level, which would add 10 ft to the allowable height.

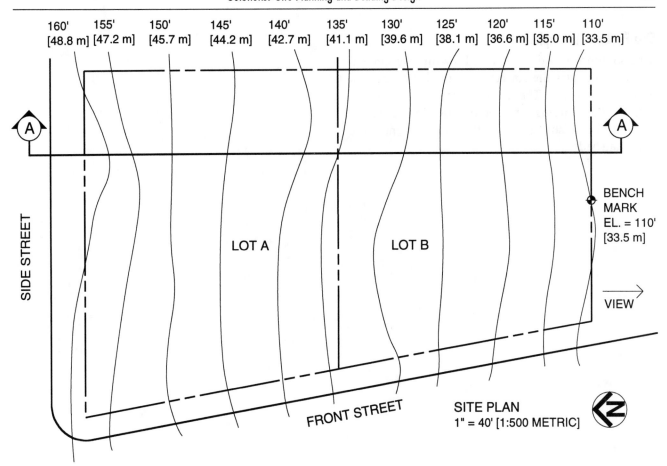

160' [48.8 m] 155' [47.2 m] 150' [45.7 m] 145' [44.2 m] 140' [42.7 m] 135' [41.1 m] 130' [39.6 m] 125' [38.1 m] 120' [36.6 m] 115' [35.0 m] 110' [33.5 m]

SIDE STREET

LOT A   LOT B

BENCH MARK
EL. = 110'
[33.5 m]

VIEW

FRONT STREET

SITE PLAN
1" = 40' [1:500 METRIC]

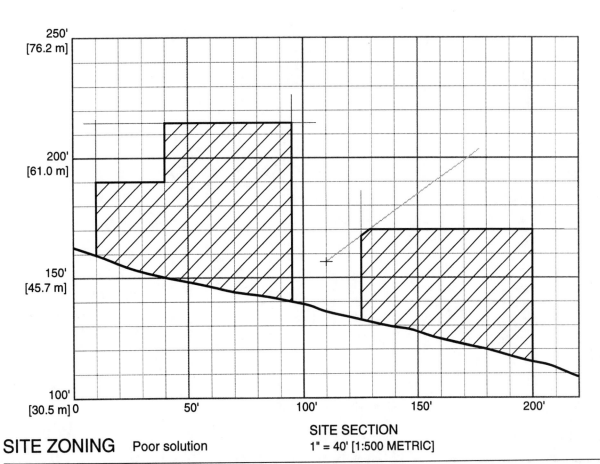

250' [76.2 m]

200' [61.0 m]

150' [45.7 m]

100' [30.5 m] 0   50'   100'   150'   200'

SITE ZONING   Poor solution

SITE SECTION
1" = 40' [1:500 METRIC]

Site Parking, Example 1

This solution provides efficient, flow-through circulation and includes the correct number of standard and accessible spaces. The accessible spaces are located close to the building, and the one tree in the middle has not been disturbed. All other requirements have been satisfied.

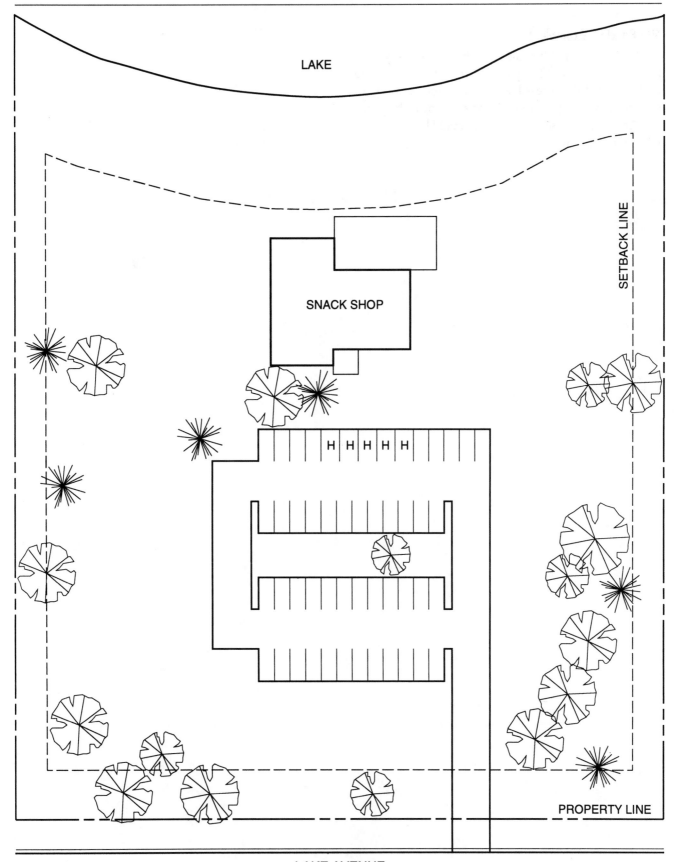

LAKE

SETBACK LINE

SNACK SHOP

H H H H H

PROPERTY LINE

LAKE AVENUE

SITE PLAN

SCALE: 1" = 60' [1:720 METRIC]

SITE PARKING   Good solution

Site Parking, Example 2

This poor solution illustrates one that could easily have been made to work. The parking area is too close to the building, and the accessible spaces are too far away. In addition, the entry drive disturbs a tree near the property line. All of these shortcomings could be eliminated with minor changes.

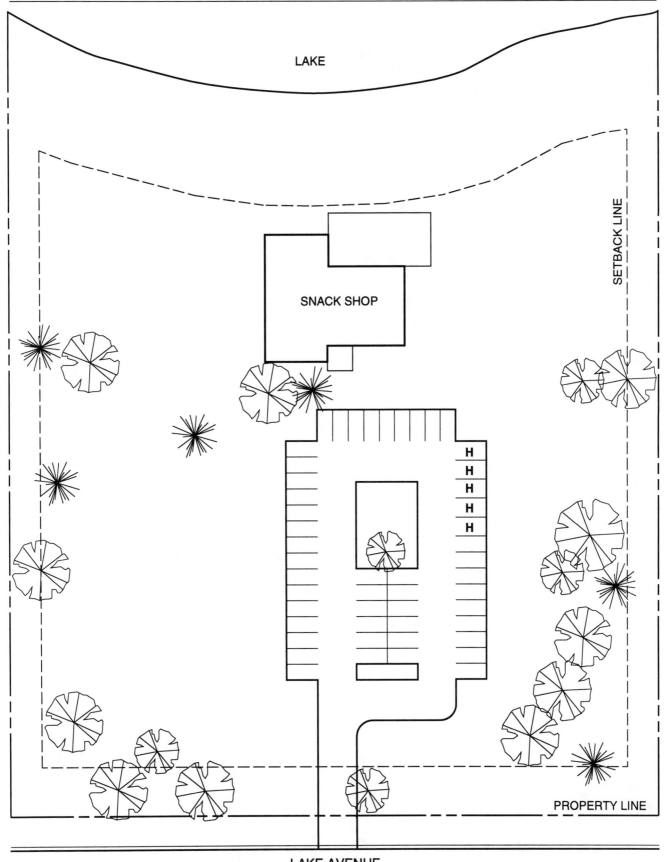

LAKE

SETBACK LINE

SNACK SHOP

H
H
H
H
H

PROPERTY LINE

LAKE AVENUE

SITE PLAN

SCALE: 1" = 60' [1:720 METRIC]

SITE PARKING Poor solution

Site Analysis, Example 1

In this solution all the setbacks are correctly indicated and the buildable area is crosshatched, including the small area north of the ditch. All restrictions have been satisfied.

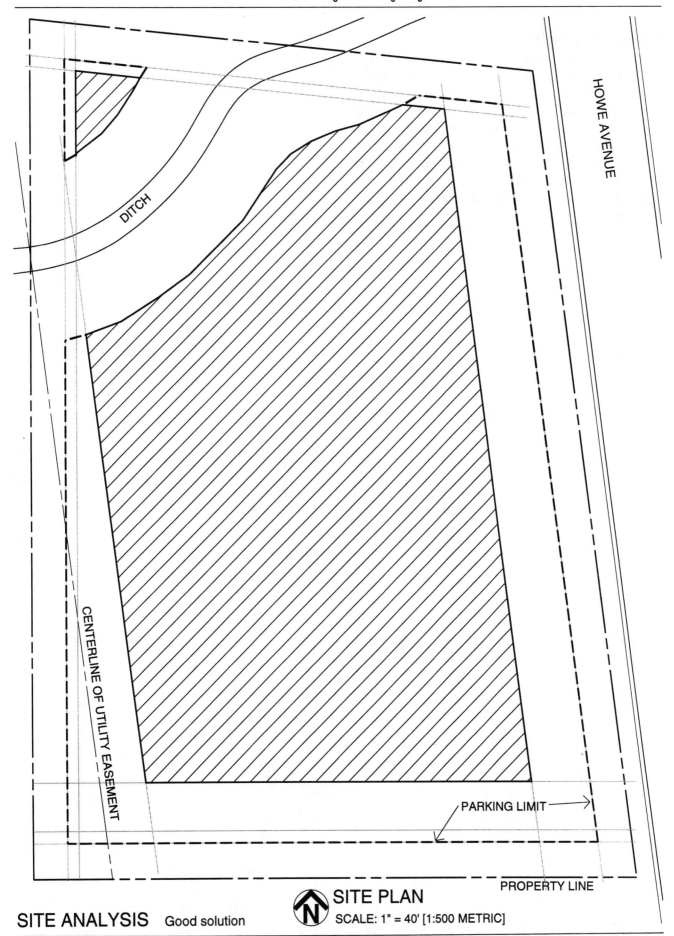

DITCH

HOWE AVENUE

CENTERLINE OF UTILITY EASEMENT

PARKING LIMIT

PROPERTY LINE

SITE PLAN
SCALE: 1" = 40' [1:500 METRIC]

SITE ANALYSIS   Good solution

Site Analysis, Example 2

There are three major problems with this solution. The utility easement is incorrectly shown as 40 ft from the centerline instead of half the required easement dimension. The parking limit on the west has been incorrectly drawn, using the utility easement center line as the measuring point instead of the property line as indicated on the program, which only prohibits buildings within the easement. Finally, the buildable area north of the ditch, even though it is small and not practical to use, should be shown.

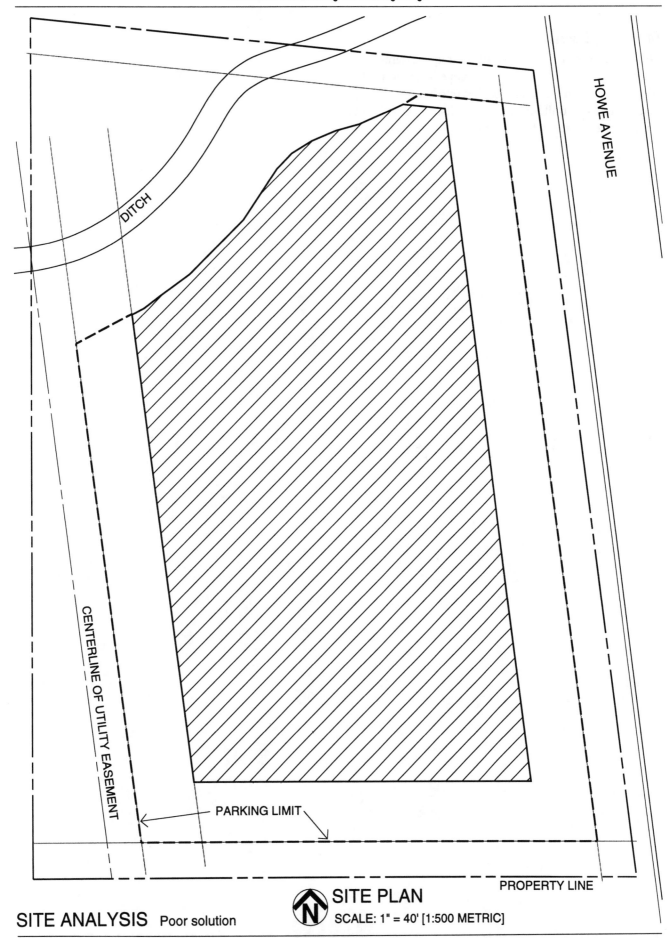

HOWE AVENUE

DITCH

CENTERLINE OF UTILITY EASEMENT

PARKING LIMIT

PROPERTY LINE

SITE ANALYSIS Poor solution

SITE PLAN
SCALE: 1" = 40' [1:500 METRIC]

Site Section, Example 1

This solution has satisfied all of the requirements, including maintaining the required slope limitations. In addition, no foundation encroaches into bedrock. Note that the office is built entirely on undisturbed soil, not on fill, as required by the program.

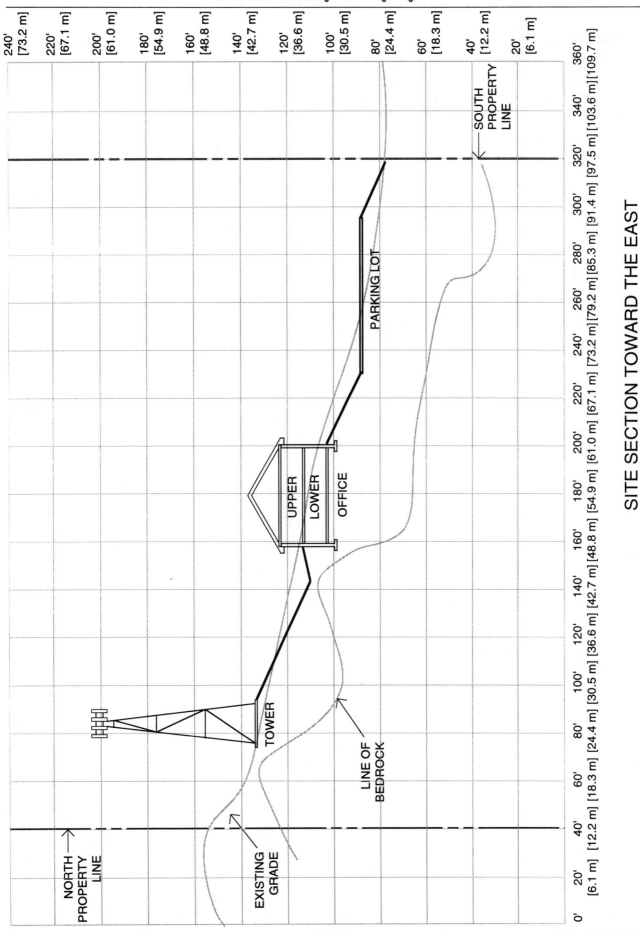

240' [73.2 m]
220' [67.1 m]
200' [61.0 m]
180' [54.9 m]
160' [48.8 m]
140' [42.7 m]
120' [36.6 m]
100' [30.5 m]
80' [24.4 m]
60' [18.3 m]
40' [12.2 m]
20' [6.1 m]

NORTH PROPERTY LINE

EXISTING GRADE

TOWER

LINE OF BEDROCK

UPPER
LOWER
OFFICE

PARKING LOT

SOUTH PROPERTY LINE

0'   20'   40'   60'   80'   100'   120'   140'   160'   180'   200'   220'   240'   260'   280'   300'   320'   340'   360'
[6.1 m] [12.2 m] [18.3 m] [24.4 m] [30.5 m] [36.6 m] [42.7 m] [48.8 m] [54.9 m] [61.0 m] [67.1 m] [73.2 m] [79.2 m] [85.3 m] [91.4 m] [97.5 m] [103.6 m] [109.7 m]

SITE SECTION   Good solution

SITE SECTION TOWARD THE EAST

SCALE: 1" = 40' [1:500 METRIC]

Site Section, Example 2

This is a fairly good solution except for two areas. The slope forces drainage into the office building on the north, and the grade outside the south property line has been disturbed to keep within the 2:1 slope limitation.

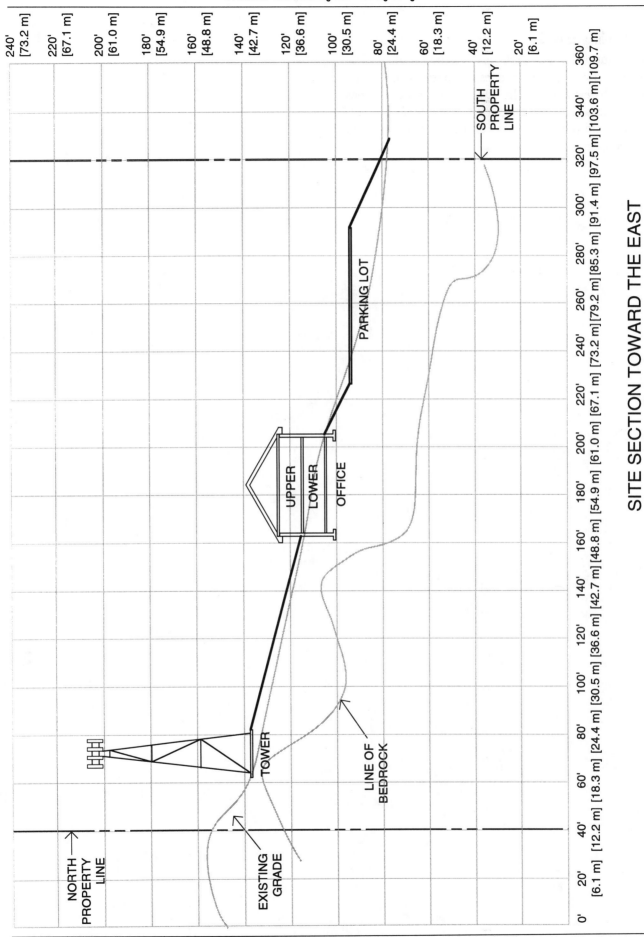

SITE SECTION TOWARD THE EAST
SCALE: 1" = 40' [1:500 METRIC]

SITE SECTION   Poor solution

Site Grading, Example 1

This solution provides adequate grading to direct water away from the patio on all four sides, including the northwest corner. The 50% slope requirement has been maintained, and the existing contours at the building line and the east portion of the site have not been changed.

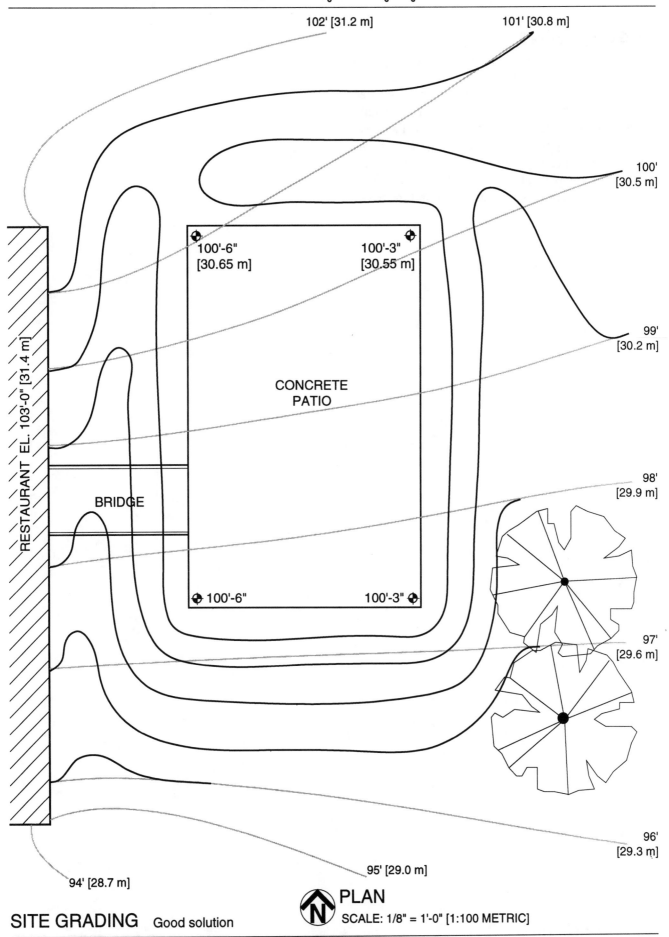

102' [31.2 m]

101' [30.8 m]

100' [30.5 m]

99' [30.2 m]

100'-6" [30.65 m]

100'-3" [30.55 m]

CONCRETE PATIO

RESTAURANT EL. 103'-0" [31.4 m]

BRIDGE

98' [29.9 m]

100'-6"

100'-3"

97' [29.6 m]

96' [29.3 m]

94' [28.7 m]

95' [29.0 m]

PLAN

N

SCALE: 1/8" = 1'-0" [1:100 METRIC]

SITE GRADING Good solution

Site Grading, Example 2

This solution has a serious flaw in the grading. The grades of 99 ft and 100 ft have not been carried around the southern portion of the patio, resulting in a steep drop-off from the patio and a requirement for retaining walls or guardrails (for safety reasons), both of which are prohibited by the program. In addition, the northwest corner of the patio is below the grade, resulting in water runoff onto the patio at this point. The tree trunks are also disturbed by excessive grading around the trees.

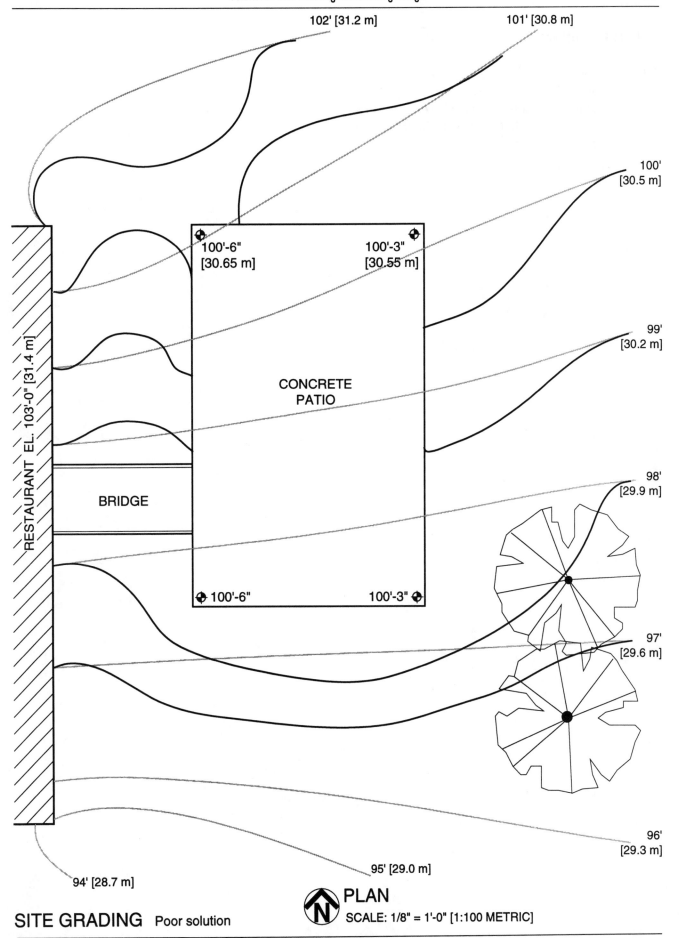

102' [31.2 m]

101' [30.8 m]

100' [30.5 m]

RESTAURANT EL. 103'-0" [31.4 m]

100'-6" [30.65 m]

100'-3" [30.55 m]

99' [30.2 m]

CONCRETE PATIO

98' [29.9 m]

BRIDGE

100'-6"

100'-3"

97' [29.6 m]

96' [29.3 m]

94' [28.7 m]

95' [29.0 m]

PLAN

SCALE: 1/8" = 1'-0" [1:100 METRIC]

SITE GRADING   Poor solution

BUILDING PLANNING

Block Diagram, Example 1

This solution has the building properly sited and oriented to existing site features. The adjacency requirements have been satisfied, and the area limitations for each space have been met.

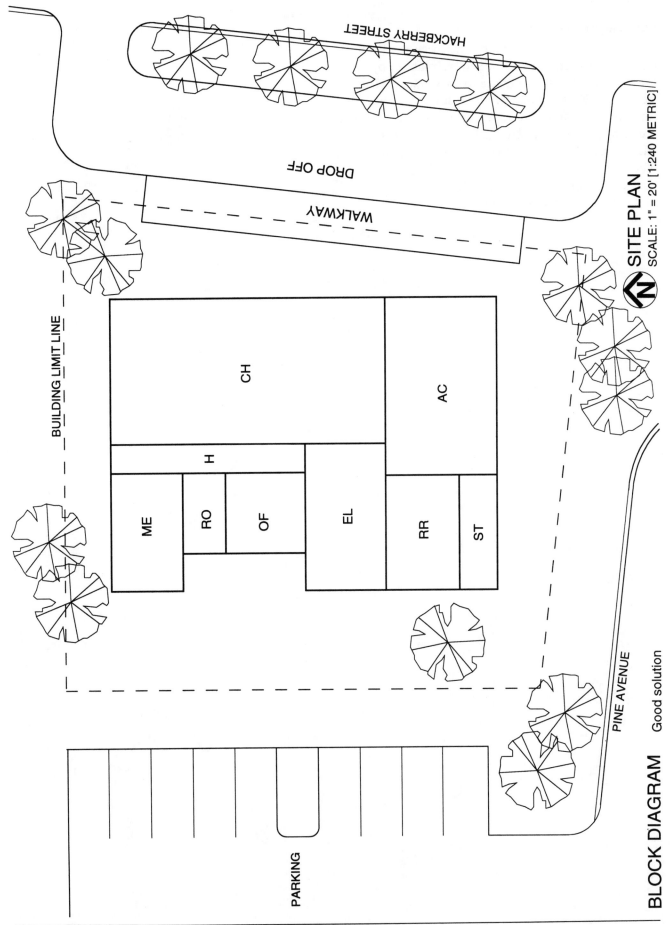

SITE PLAN
SCALE: 1" = 20' [1:240 METRIC]

HACKBERRY STREET

DROP OFF

WALKWAY

BUILDING LIMIT LINE

CH

AC

H

ME

RO

OF

EL

RR

ST

PINE AVENUE

PARKING

BLOCK DIAGRAM   Good solution

Block Diagram, Example 2

In this solution the building has not been sited well. One tree has been removed, which is prohibited by the program, and the side entrance to the chapel does not face the parking drop-off on the east side. Although this is a minor problem because the drop-off area is still accessible, it would be better to have direct access. The chapel entrance is not adjacent to the lobby, and the office is a little too small. Conversely, the lobby is on the extreme upper limit in area. (Try to be within 10% of the stated area requirements.)

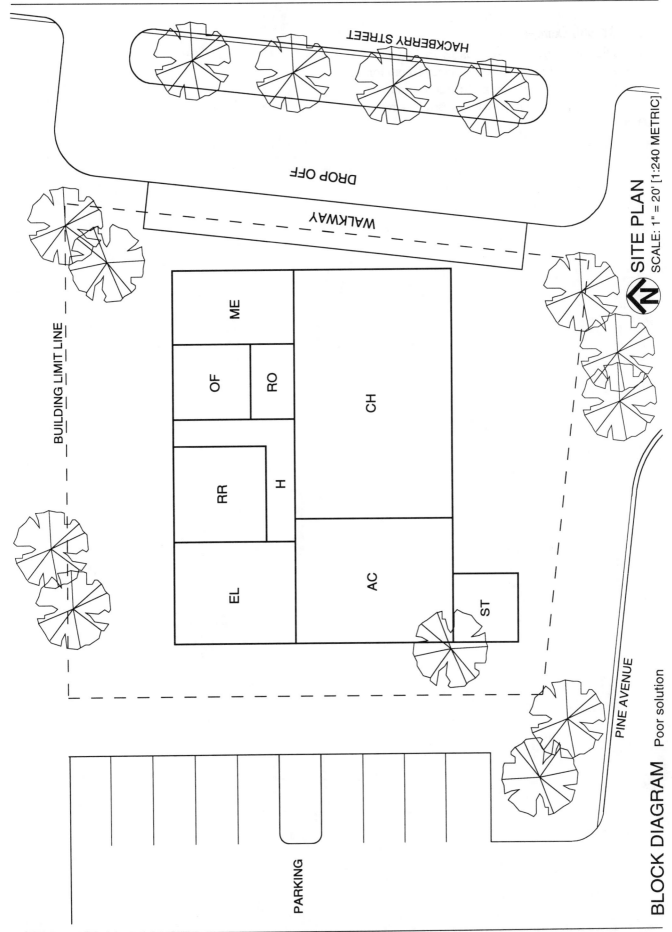

HACKBERRY STREET

DROP OFF

WALKWAY

BUILDING LIMIT LINE

ME

OF

RO

CH

RR

H

EL

AC

ST

PINE AVENUE

PARKING

SITE PLAN
SCALE: 1" = 20' [1:240 METRIC]

BLOCK DIAGRAM Poor solution

Interior Layout, Example 1

In this solution all the required spaces are laid out in a logical and efficient manner with sufficient room for all the furniture. Clearances around furniture and maneuvering clearances at doors satisfy accessibility requirements.

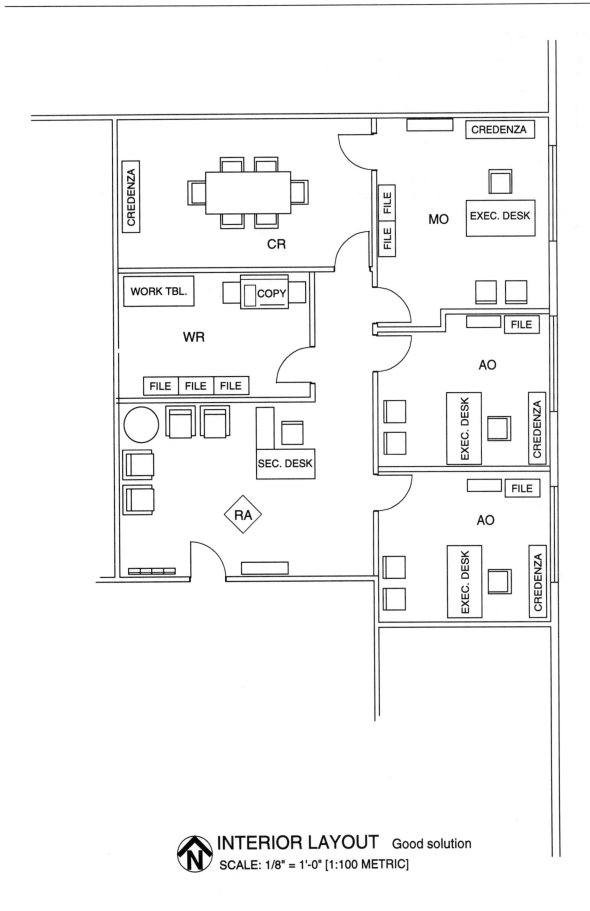

INTERIOR LAYOUT Good solution
SCALE: 1/8" = 1'-0" [1:100 METRIC]

Interior Layout, Example 2

In this solution several program requirements have been violated. There is no direct access (doorway) between the manager's office and conference room. There is insufficient space for accessibility at the door to the manager's office, the bookcase encroaches into the space inside the office, and there is not enough space on the strike side of the door on the outside of the door. The lounge chairs are too close to the wall of the conference room for accessibility, and the space in the workroom is too tight. Finally, the display rack is missing from the reception area.

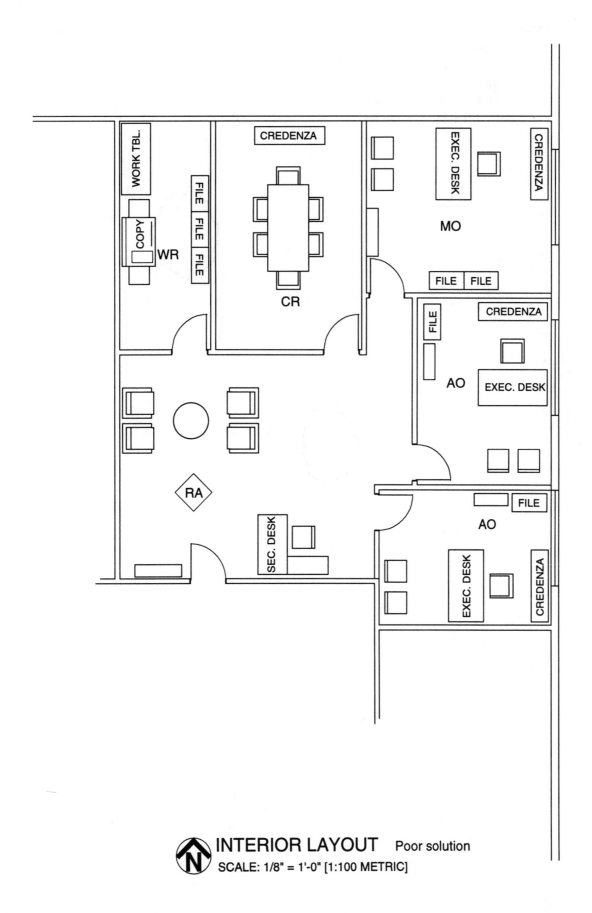

WORK TBL.

COPY

WR

FILE FILE FILE

CREDENZA

CR

EXEC. DESK

MO

CREDENZA

FILE FILE

FILE

CREDENZA

AO

EXEC. DESK

RA

SEC. DESK

FILE

AO

EXEC. DESK

CREDENZA

INTERIOR LAYOUT   Poor solution
N   SCALE: 1/8" = 1'-0" [1:100 METRIC]

Schematic Design, Example 1

In this good solution the building has been oriented on the site to satisfy all program requirements. The organization of both first- and second-floor plans is logical and direct. All spaces are included and are within the areas stipulated in the program. All exiting requirements have been satisfied.

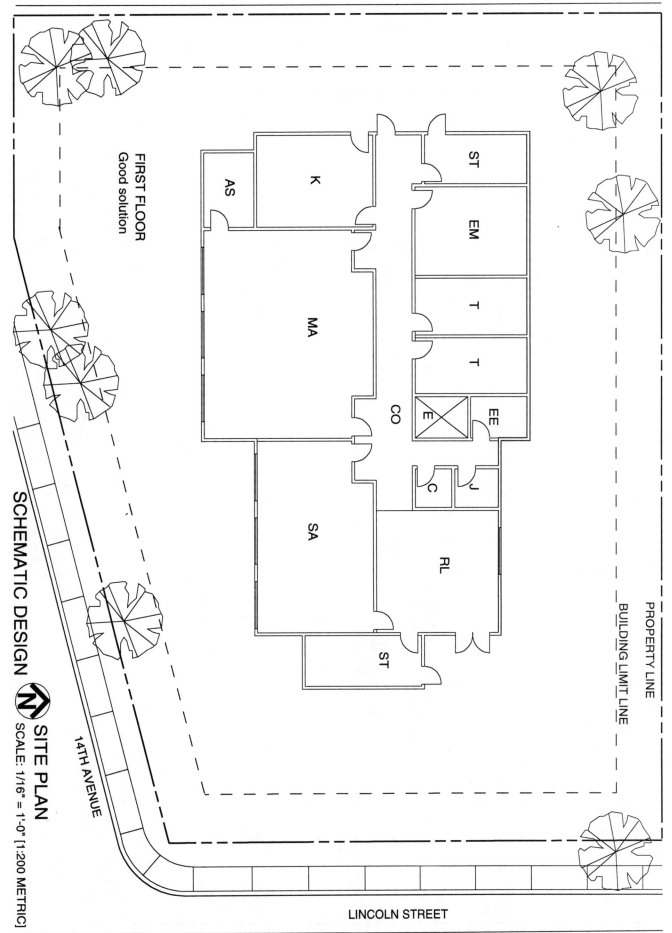

FIRST FLOOR
Good solution

SCHEMATIC DESIGN

SITE PLAN
SCALE: 1/16" = 1'-0" [1:200 METRIC]

14TH AVENUE

LINCOLN STREET

PROPERTY LINE
BUILDING LIMIT LINE

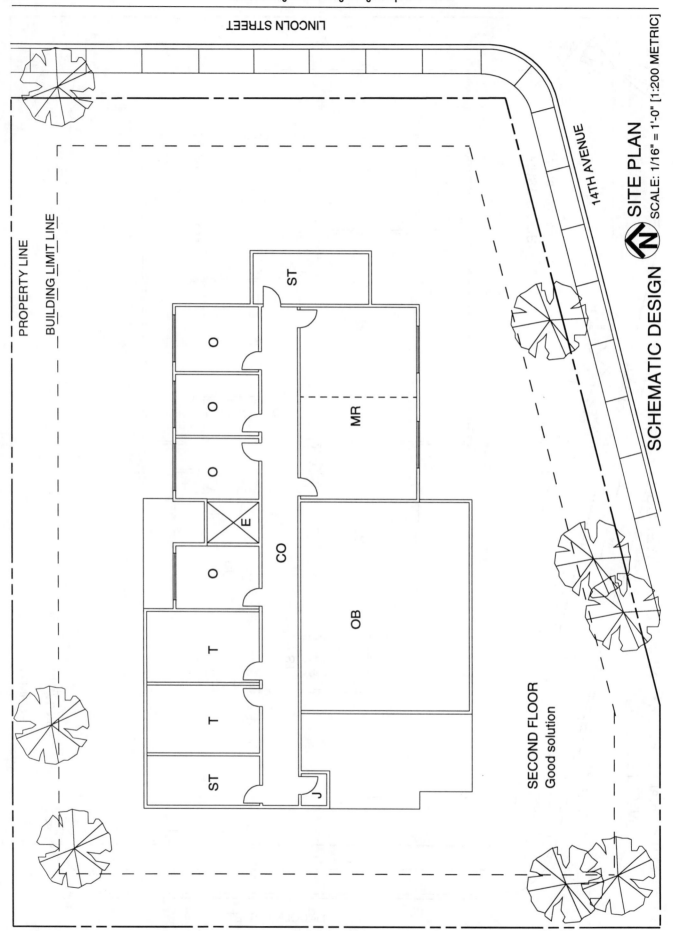

LINCOLN STREET

PROPERTY LINE

BUILDING LIMIT LINE

14TH AVENUE

SITE PLAN

SCALE: 1/16" = 1'-0" [1:200 METRIC]

SCHEMATIC DESIGN

ST

O O O

E

T T O

ST T

J

CO

MR

OB

SECOND FLOOR
Good solution

Schematic Design, Example 2

The general organization of this poor solution is awkward and results in several violations of the program. On the first floor there is no door from the kitchen to the corridor. The corridor to the toilet rooms is less than the 6 ft required by the program. There is also a major exiting mistake: the two doors from the senior activities room are too close together and they swing in.

On the second floor the layout of the offices is not logical. This may be considered a minor problem, but a more significant problem is that one office is too large and two offices are too small. The large office also lacks a window. The orientation of the meeting room requires that when the room is subdivided there is not a separate exit as required by the program.

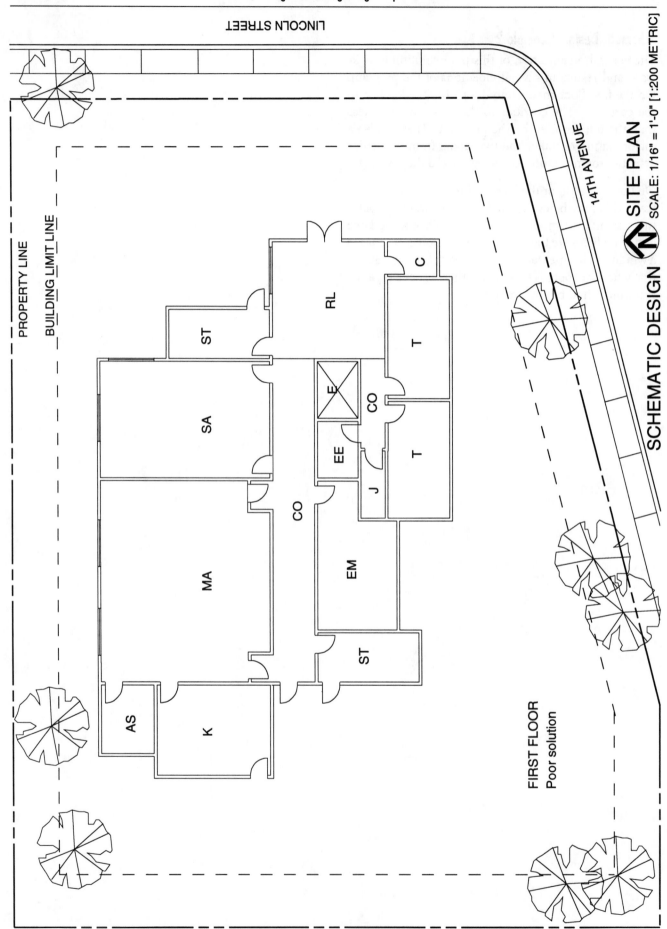

LINCOLN STREET

14TH AVENUE

PROPERTY LINE

BUILDING LIMIT LINE

AS

K

MA

SA

ST

CO

RL

EM

ST

EE

E

CO

J

T

T

CO

C

FIRST FLOOR
Poor solution

SITE PLAN
SCHEMATIC DESIGN
SCALE: 1/16" = 1'-0" [1:200 METRIC]

N

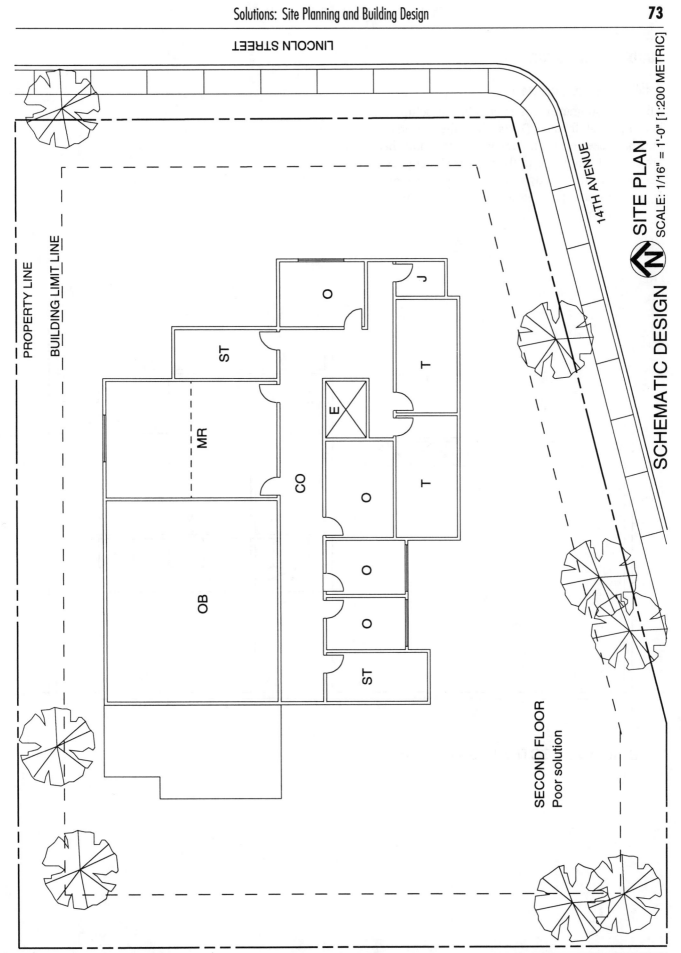

SITE PLAN
SCALE: 1/16" = 1'-0" [1:200 METRIC]

SCHEMATIC DESIGN

LINCOLN STREET

14TH AVENUE

PROPERTY LINE

BUILDING LIMIT LINE

OB

MR

ST

CO

O

O

O

E

T

T

J

O

ST

SECOND FLOOR
Poor solution

BUILDING TECHNOLOGY

Building Section, Example 1

All of the program requirements in this solution have been successfully met. Ducts where the section cut occurs have been drawn to the correct size, ceiling heights are correctly shown, and the structural members have been indicated correctly and in the proper position. The foundations and parapets are also shown correctly.

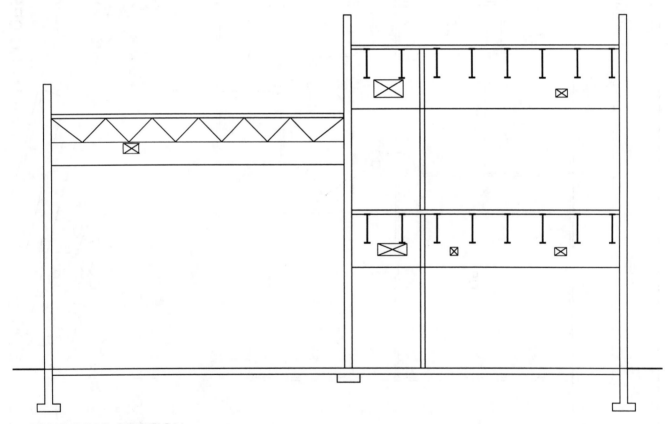

BUILDING SECTION—Good solution

Building Section, Example 2

This solution has several faults. The interior footing is shown too low. Because it is an interior footing, it does not have to be at frost depth as the outside footings do. The corridor partition does not extend to the deck above on both the first and second floors as it must do if it is a fire-rated partition. On the first floor the 8 in. × 8 in. duct is drawn too large. On the second floor there is not enough room below the large duct for light fixtures.

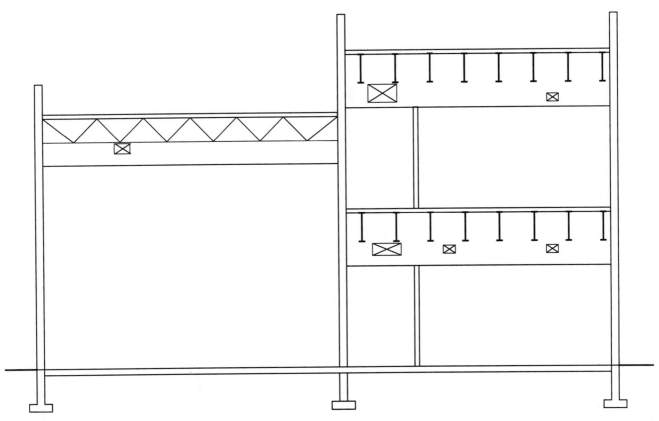

BUILDING SECTION—Poor solution

Structural Layout, Example 1

This solution provides an efficient structural system that satisfies all the requirements. Columns placed on the bearing wall provide for the required clerestory window above the service bay. Joist spacing does not exceed the limits of the program, and all bearing walls, beams, and lintels are properly indicated.

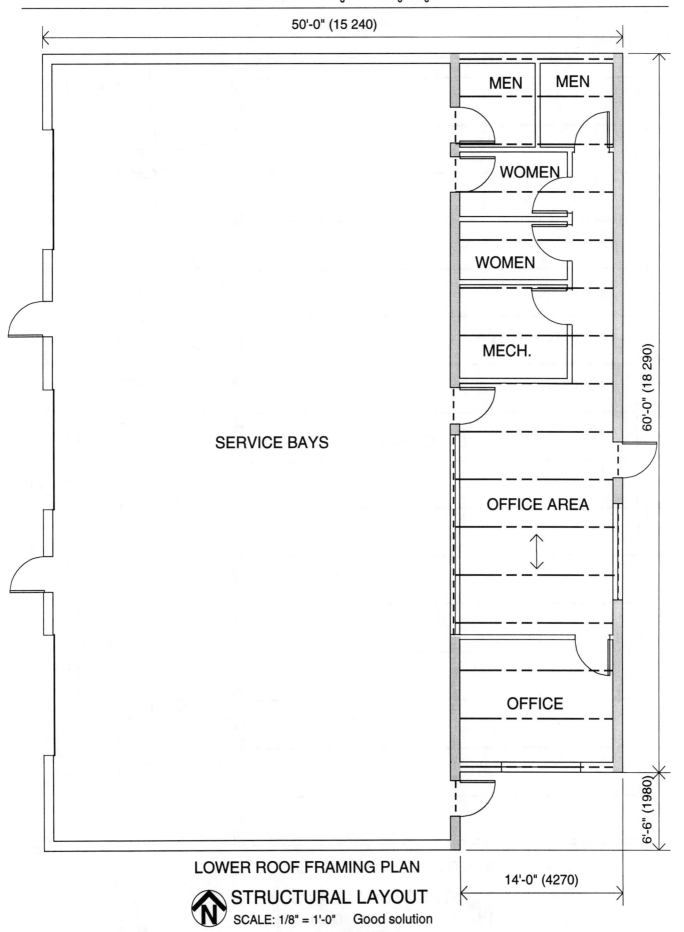

50'-0" (15 240)

MEN MEN

WOMEN

WOMEN

MECH.

SERVICE BAYS

60'-0" (18 290)

OFFICE AREA

OFFICE

6'-6" (1980)

LOWER ROOF FRAMING PLAN

STRUCTURAL LAYOUT

N

SCALE: 1/8" = 1'-0"   Good solution

14'-0" (4270)

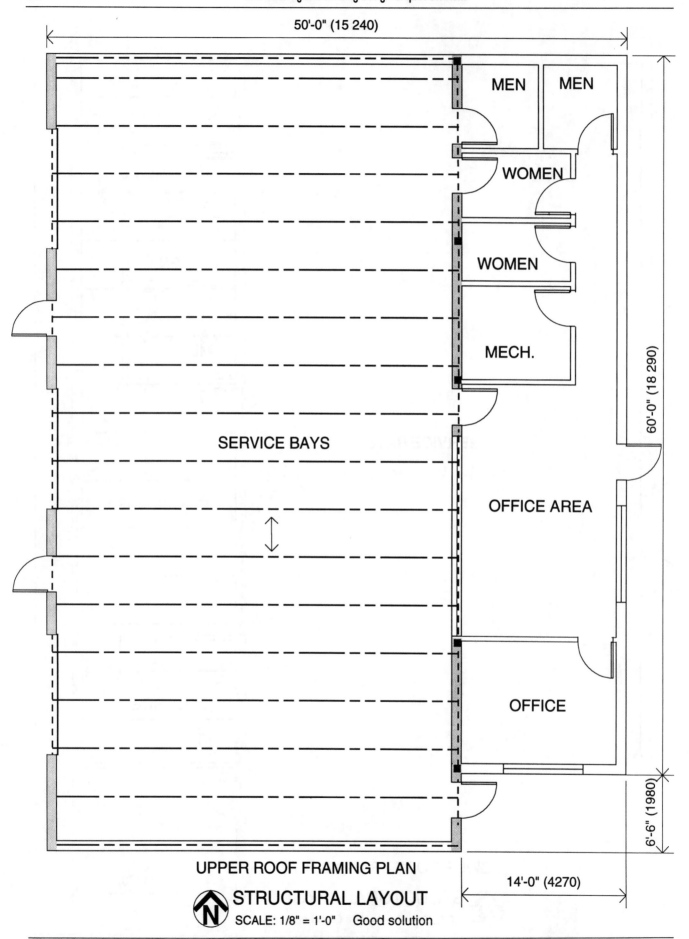

50'-0" (15 240)

MEN   MEN

WOMEN

WOMEN

MECH.

SERVICE BAYS

OFFICE AREA

OFFICE

60'-0" (18 290)

6'-6" (1980)

14'-0" (4270)

UPPER ROOF FRAMING PLAN

STRUCTURAL LAYOUT

N   SCALE: 1/8" = 1'-0"   Good solution

Structural Layout, Example 2

The major mistake on the first level of this solution is that the joist spacing exceeds the 4'-0" span capacity of the decking as stated in the program. In addition, the columns shown on the second-floor plan are not shown on this plan.

On the second floor the structural system over the service bays is not efficient because the beams span the long direction relative to the joists. Also, the column at the office area would have to either bear on a beam over the glass between the office area and service bays area or extend through the opening.

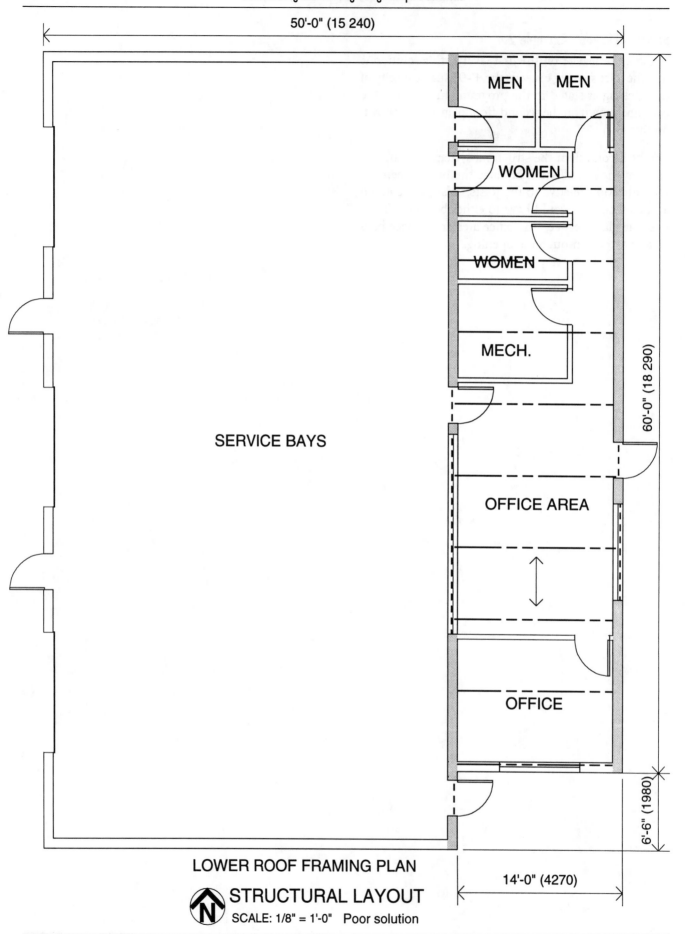

50'-0" (15 240)

60'-0" (18 290)

6'-6" (1980)

14'-0" (4270)

MEN

MEN

WOMEN

WOMEN

MECH.

SERVICE BAYS

OFFICE AREA

OFFICE

LOWER ROOF FRAMING PLAN

STRUCTURAL LAYOUT

N

SCALE: 1/8" = 1'-0"   Poor solution

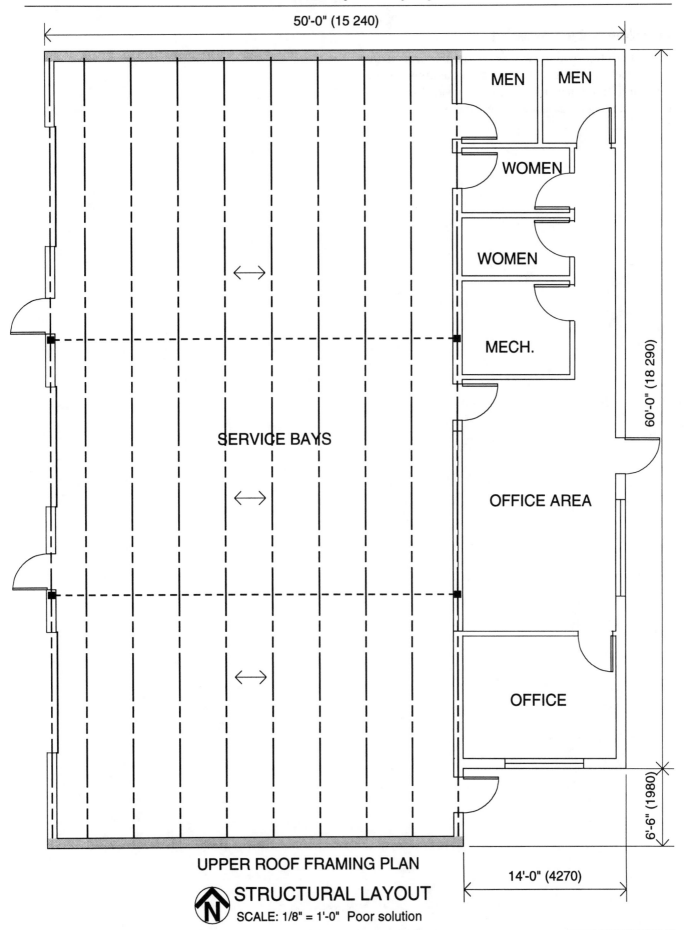

50'-0" (15 240)

MEN   MEN

WOMEN

WOMEN

MECH.

60'-0" (18 290)

SERVICE BAYS

OFFICE AREA

OFFICE

6'-6" (1980)

UPPER ROOF FRAMING PLAN

STRUCTURAL LAYOUT

SCALE: 1/8" = 1'-0" Poor solution

14'-0" (4270)

Accessibility—Ramp, Example 1

This solution provides a simple, straightforward method of meeting all the requirements of the program. All ramp and stair dimensions are properly established, and there is enough clearance at the side of the door for accessibility.

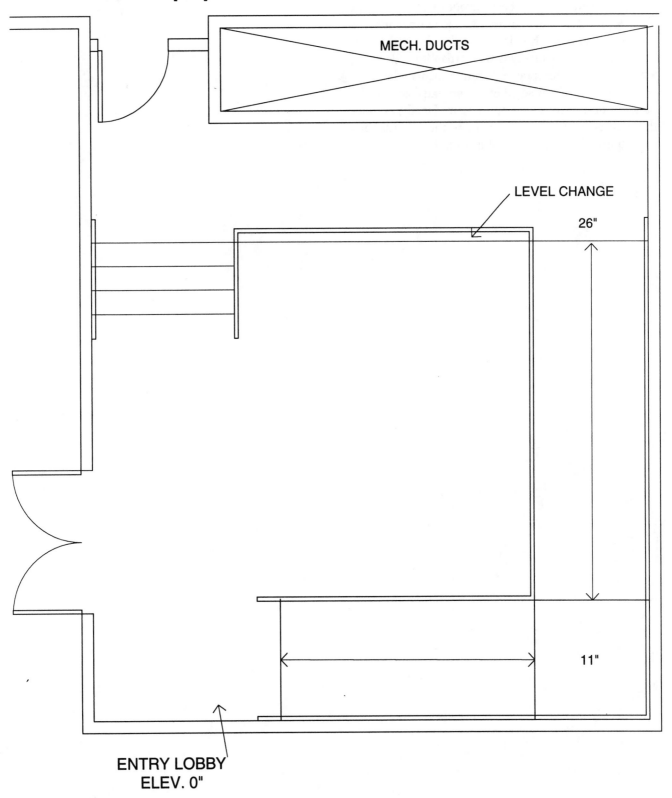

EXIT CORRIDOR
ELEV. 26" [660]

MECH. DUCTS

LEVEL CHANGE

26"

11"

ENTRY LOBBY
ELEV. 0"

ACCESSIBILITY—RAMP Good solution
SCALE: 1/4" = 1'-0" [1:50 METRIC]

Accessibility—Ramp, Example 2

This poor solution has a basic layout that would work if a few problems were corrected. The ramp landing is only 4 ft deep, which is less than the required 60 in. The width of the stairway is wider than it needs to be, which would be acceptable if an intermediate handrail had been shown. Also, there is no extension of the handrail on the west side of the stair. Finally, because the door is centered in the opening, there is less than the required 18 in. for accessibility on the strike side of the door.

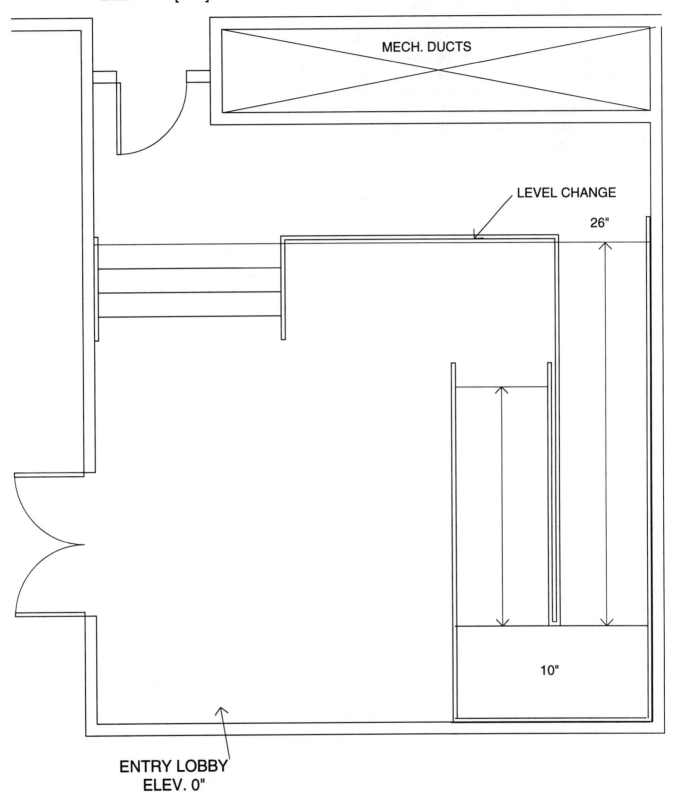

EXIT CORRIDOR
ELEV. 26" [660]

MECH. DUCTS

LEVEL CHANGE

26"

10"

ENTRY LOBBY
ELEV. 0"

ACCESSIBILITY—RAMP Poor solution
SCALE: 1/4" = 1'-0" [1:50 METRIC]

Mechanical and Electrical Plan, Example 1

All of the requirements listed in the program are met with this solution. The grid in each room is centered to provide for uniform illumination, and the rigid duct is located to coordinate with the structure. One aspect of this vignette requiring care is the proper spacing of light fixtures. Look at the lighting diagrams to see what the maximum beam spread is for the required illumination level. Also, be careful to limit the length of flexible duct to that required by the program.

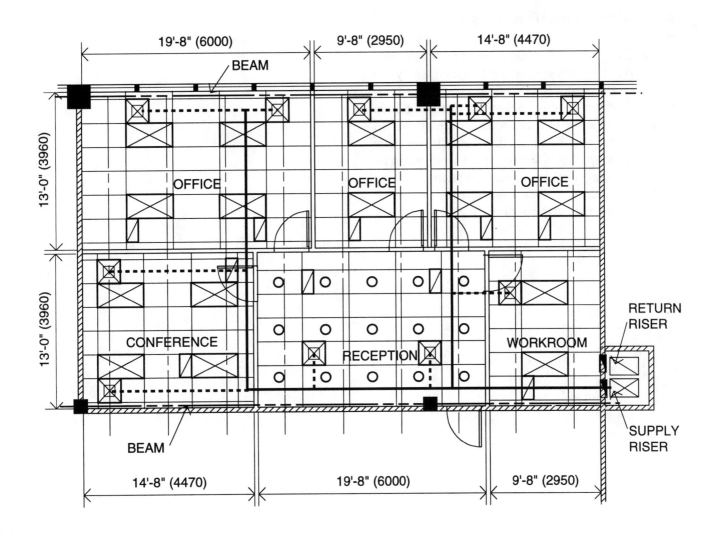

	Recessed fluorescent fixture
	Recessed incandescent fixture
	Supply air diffuser
	Return air grille
——	Rigid supply duct
- - - - -	Flexible supply duct
/////	Fire-rated wall
— · —	Bar joist
◤	Fire damper

MECHANICAL AND ELECTRICAL PLAN
SCALE: 1/8" = 1'-0" [1:100 metric]   Good solution

Mechanical and Electrical Plan, Example 2

In this solution the length of the rigid duct is excessive, and one of the flexible ducts in the conference room serves two diffusers, which is prohibited by the program. There is only one return grille in the large office and only one supply diffuser and return grille in the smaller office in the east portion of the suite. In the large office and the small office there are too many light fixtures (spacing is less than the 4 ft suggested by the lighting diagrams) and in the reception area there are too few lights. The east-west spacing (at 4 ft) is acceptable, but the north-south spacing is too far apart.

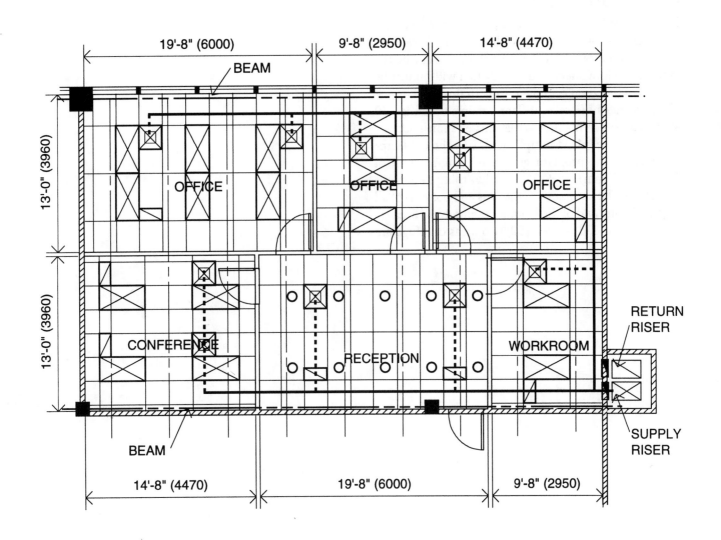

Recessed fluorescent fixture

O   Recessed incandescent fixture

Supply air diffuser

Return air grille

———   Rigid supply duct

- - - - - -   Flexible supply duct

////////   Fire-rated wall

— · —   Bar joist

Fire damper

MECHANICAL AND ELECTRICAL PLAN
SCALE: 1/8" = 1'-0" [1:100 metric]   Poor solution

Stair Design, Example 1

This solution meets all of the requirements of the program. One of the first things to check with this vignette is the minimum width of the exit stairs. It may be the minimum width stated, but more often width must be calculated based on occupant load. In this vignette the program states the second-floor occupant load is 340 with two exits. This means that this exit must accommodate 170 people. Multiplying this by the 0.3 factor as stated in the program gives a minimum width of 51 in. (1295 mm), or 4'-3". Another thing to remember is to set the elevations of the tops and bottoms of all flights of stairs and of the landings themselves. Because the occupant load is over 150, two areas of refuge are required.

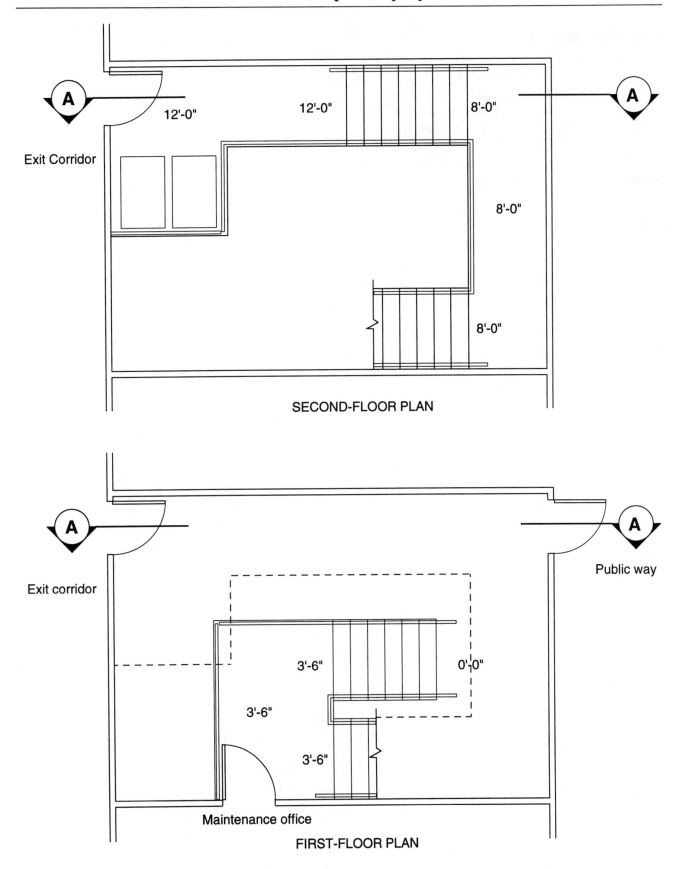

SECOND-FLOOR PLAN

FIRST-FLOOR PLAN

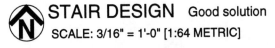

STAIR DESIGN   Good solution
SCALE: 3/16" = 1'-0" [1:64 METRIC]

Stair Design, Example 2

This solution illustrates some of the common mistakes made in this vignette. The landing at 7'-6" (2290 mm) is a little too low for adequate headroom below. Because the program states the precast structure is 12 in. (305 mm) deep, this would leave headroom of 6'-6" (1980 mm), 2 in. short of the minimum 80 in. (2030 mm). There is also no handrail on the north side of the upper flight of stairs.

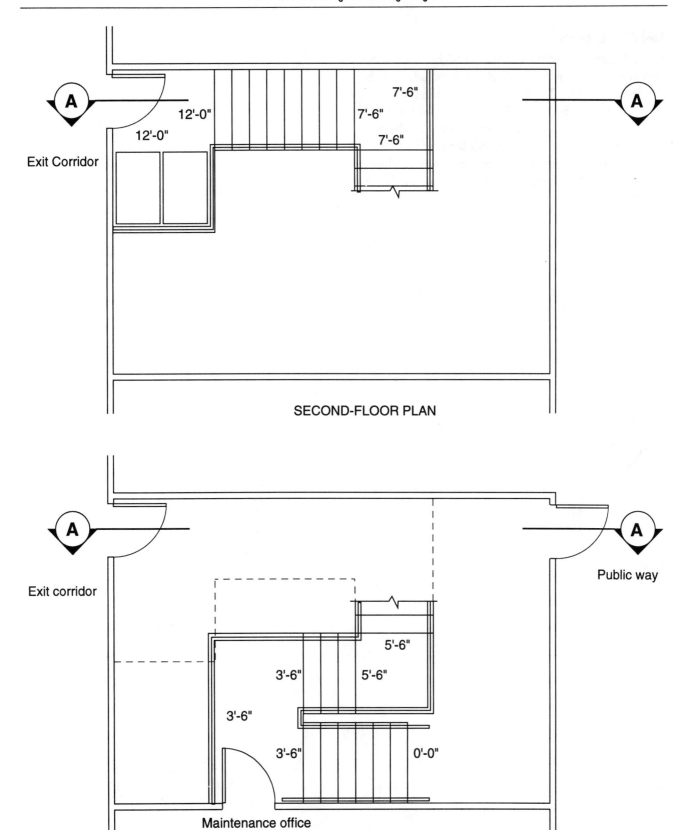

SECOND-FLOOR PLAN

FIRST-FLOOR PLAN

STAIR DESIGN Poor solution
SCALE: 3/16" = 1'-0" [1:64 METRIC]

Roof Plan, Example 1

This solution represents a simple, straightforward roof plan that sheds water effectively and includes all the required elements. The low portions of the lower roof are set at 9'-6" (2895 mm), which allows for the 18 in. (457 mm) structural depth. The slope meets the program limitations and still provides for adequate space for the 30 in. (760 mm) high clerestory. All water drains into gutters, which connect to properly located downspouts.

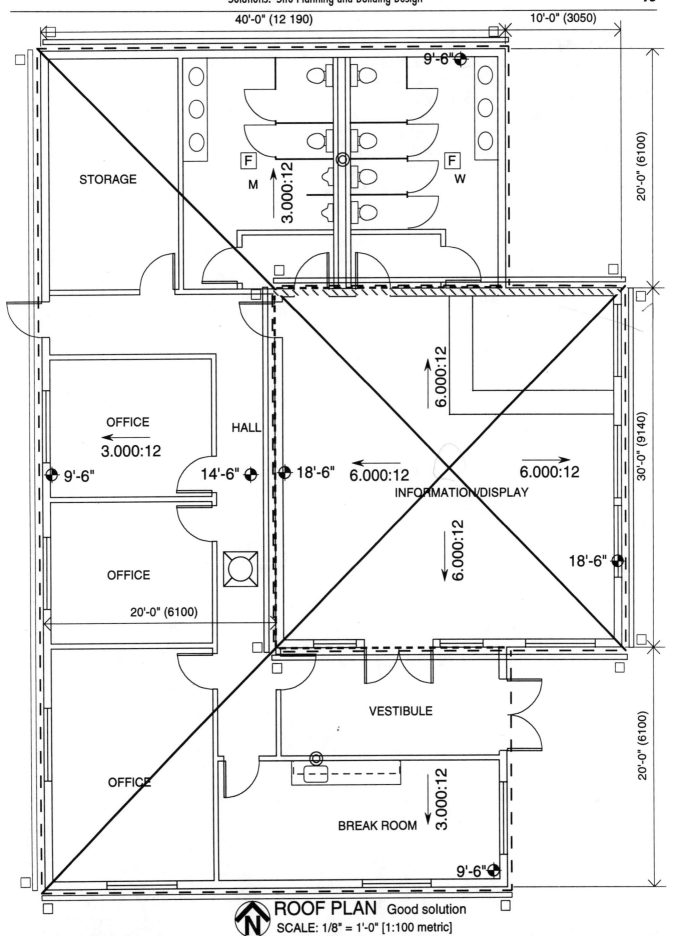

40'-0" (12 190)   10'-0" (3050)

20'-0" (6100)

30'-0" (9140)

20'-0" (6100)

STORAGE

9'-6"

F
M

3.000:12

F
W

HALL

OFFICE
3.000:12

9'-6"

14'-6"   18'-6"

6.000:12

6.000:12

6.000:12   6.000:12

INFORMATION/DISPLAY

6.000:12

18'-6"

OFFICE

OFFICE

20'-0" (6100)

VESTIBULE

OFFICE

BREAK ROOM

3.000:12

9'-6"

ROOF PLAN Good solution
N SCALE: 1/8" = 1'-0" [1:100 metric]

Roof Plan, Example 2

The gable roof layout for this solution is adequate, but the elevations are set incorrectly. First, the 8'-0" lower elevation of the lower roof does not allow for roof structure. Second, the lower roof slope and the elevation of the lower portion of the upper roof structure do not allow sufficient room for the clerestory and upper roof structure. Gutters are missing to catch rainwater draining from the upper roof to the lower roof, and the vent for the break room sink is missing.

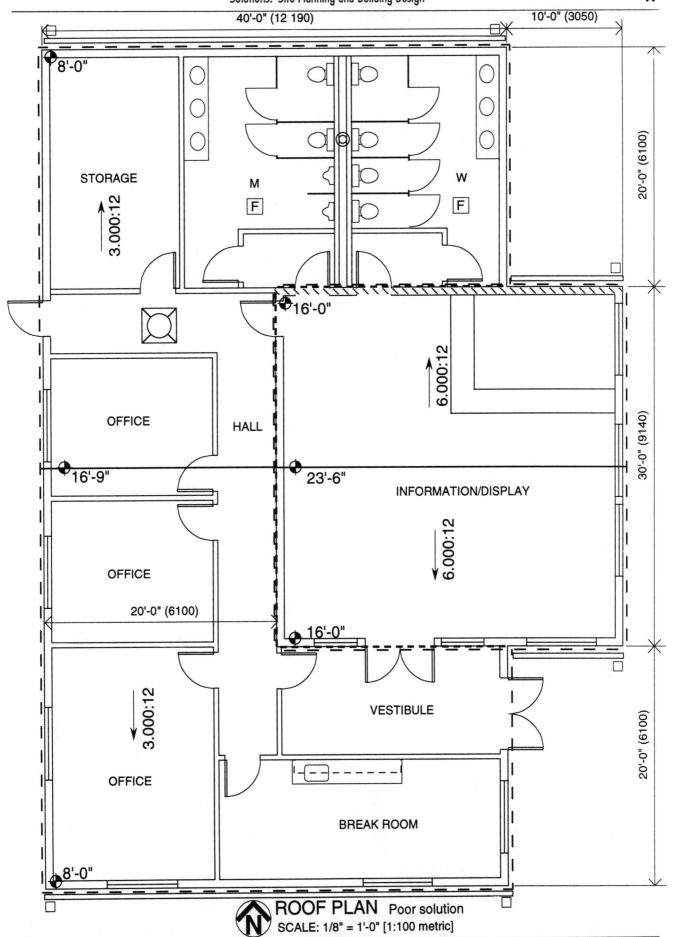

40'-0" (12 190)

10'-0" (3050)

20'-0" (6100)

8'-0"

STORAGE

3.000:12

M

F

W

F

16'-0"

6.000:12

OFFICE

HALL

INFORMATION/DISPLAY

30'-0" (9140)

16'-9"

23'-6"

6.000:12

OFFICE

20'-0" (6100)

16'-0"

3.000:12

VESTIBULE

20'-0" (6100)

OFFICE

BREAK ROOM

8'-0"

ROOF PLAN Poor solution
SCALE: 1/8" = 1'-0" [1:100 metric]

N